Transform Your Problems into Opportunities: Learn to Give a 180-Degree Spin to your Challenges

TRANSFORM YOUR PROBLEMS INTO OPPORTUNITIES

First edition. March 14, 2024.

ISBN: 979-8224298105

Written by Gonzalo Estrada.

Table of Contents

Contents

Chapter 1: Understanding the Power of Perception

Explore how your perception shapes your reality and how shifting it can help you see challenges as opportunities.

Perception is a powerful force that drives our thoughts, emotions, and actions. It is the lens through which we view the world, coloring our experiences and shaping our reality. As entrepreneurs, it is vital for us to understand the profound impact that our perception can have on how we navigate the challenges that come our way.

At its core, perception is a process of interpreting and making sense of the information we receive from our senses. It goes beyond the mere act of seeing, hearing, or feeling; it involves organizing and assigning meaning to those sensory inputs. Think of it as the mental filter through which we process and understand the world around us.

What makes perception fascinating is that it is not a fixed, immutable trait. It is malleable and subject to change. Our perception can be influenced by various factors such as beliefs, attitudes, past experiences, and cultural influences. This malleability opens up a world of possibilities for us as entrepreneurs, as it means we have the power to shape and mold our perception to serve us in the face of challenges.

Have you ever noticed how different people can have drastically different interpretations of the same situation? One person may see an obstacle as an insurmountable roadblock, while another may view it as a chance to learn and grow. This difference in perception can mean the distinction between feeling defeated or feeling inspired.

The way we perceive challenges is often rooted in our mindset. A fixed mindset believes that abilities and intelligence are predetermined and unchangeable, leading to a fear of failure and a reluctance to take risks. On the other hand, a growth mindset sees challenges as opportunities for learning and development, embracing failure as a stepping stone to success.

Shifting our perception from a fixed mindset to a growth mindset can be a transformative experience. It allows us to see challenges not as threats, but as potential avenues for growth and innovation. Instead of being paralyzed by fear, we become energized by the possibilities that lie within each challenge.

One way to shift our perception is by practicing reframing. Reframing involves consciously changing the way we interpret a situation, finding new and empowering meanings within it. For example, instead of seeing a setback as a failure, we can reframe it as an opportunity to reassess our approach and come back stronger.

Another powerful technique is cultivating gratitude. When we focus on what we are grateful for, we train our minds to see the positive aspects of any situation. This allows us to shift our perception from dwelling on the challenges to appreciating the lessons and opportunities they present.

As entrepreneurs, we face a unique set of challenges on our journey. Uncertainty, competition, and the pressure to succeed can feel overwhelming at times. However, it is important to remember that our perception holds the key to transforming these challenges into opportunities.

By deliberately choosing to see challenges through a new lens, we invite innovation, creativity, and resilience into our entrepreneurial endeavors. We begin to see setbacks as valuable learning experiences, stepping stones on the path to success. We uncover hidden opportunities, overlooked by those who see challenges as insurmountable obstacles.

In the second half of this chapter, we will delve deeper into practical strategies to shift our perception and harness its power to transform challenges into opportunities. We will explore case studies of successful entrepreneurs who have embraced the power of perception and made it their ally. Stay tuned, as we unlock the secrets to turning your entrepreneurial challenges into stepping stones towards your ultimate success. The adventure awaits!

Shifting our perception and harnessing its power to transform challenges into opportunities is a journey that requires consistent practice and dedication. In the second half of this chapter, we will explore practical strategies and real-life examples of successful entrepreneurs who have embraced the power of perception to make it their ally.

One powerful strategy to shift our perception is through the practice of mindfulness. Mindfulness allows us to observe our thoughts, emotions, and sensations without judgment, enabling us to gain a deeper understanding of our automatic reactions and biases. By cultivating mindfulness, we can develop the ability to recognize when our perception is clouded by negativity or limiting beliefs. Through this awareness, we can intentionally choose to shift our focus towards more empowering and optimistic perspectives.

Take, for instance, the story of Sarah, an entrepreneur who was facing a major setback in her business. An unexpected financial crisis had left her in a position where she feared losing everything, she had worked so hard to build. Initially, Sarah felt overwhelmed by fear and hopelessness, perceiving this crisis as a sign of failure. However, through mindfulness practice, she learned to observe her thoughts and emotions without attachment. This allowed her to question her initial perception and look for hidden opportunities within the challenge.

Sarah reframed her situation, choosing to see the financial crisis as a wake-up call and an opportunity to reassess her business model. She realized that this setback was an invitation to innovate and explore new strategies. With a shift in perception, Sarah reimagined her business, identifying untapped markets and pursuing creative collaborations. Within a year, her business not only recovered but flourished, reaching new heights she had never imagined. Sarah's story is a testament to the transformative power of shifting our perception through mindfulness practice.

Another effective strategy to transform challenges into opportunities is by surrounding ourselves with a supportive network. The people we choose to spend time with can play a significant role in shaping our perception. When we surround ourselves with like-minded individuals who share our entrepreneurial spirit, we create an environment that nurtures growth and resilience.

Consider the example of James, an aspiring entrepreneur who faced constant skepticism from his family and friends. Initially, James allowed their doubts to influence his perception, questioning his dreams and capabilities. However, he made a conscious decision to expand his network and connect with other entrepreneurs who believed in the power of their visions. By surrounding himself with individuals who saw challenges as opportunities, James was able to shift his perception and regain the confidence needed to pursue his entrepreneurial endeavors. Today, he runs a successful business and credits his supportive network for helping him overcome his initial doubts.

By cultivating mindfulness, reframing challenges, and surrounding ourselves with a supportive network, we can gradually shift our perception and embrace the transformative power it holds. As entrepreneurs, we must remember that challenges are not roadblocks but stepping stones on our journey to success. They push us to think outside the box, innovate, and cultivate resilience.

As we continue to explore the power of perception in the subsequent chapters of this book, we will delve deeper into practical strategies, case studies, and expert insights. Together, we will unlock the secrets of how perception shapes our entrepreneurial path and learn to give a 180-degree spin to our challenges.

Remember, fellow entrepreneurs, the adventure of transforming problems into opportunities awaits us. With each shift in perception, we pave the way for our ultimate success. Let us embark on this journey with enthusiasm, determination, and the unwavering belief that challenges are not obstacles but stepping stones towards our dreams. Embrace the power of perception, and together, let us flourish in the face of every challenge that comes our way.

Chapter 2: Embracing a Growth Mindset

Discover the importance of cultivating a growth mindset to effectively navigate and overcome obstacles.

In the journey of entrepreneurship, challenges and obstacles are not just inevitable; they are essential. They serve as the stepping stones that lead us towards growth, success, and ultimately, our fullest potential. However, navigating through these hurdles requires more than just determination and perseverance; it necessitates the cultivation of a growth mindset.

A growth mindset is a powerful mindset shift that allows us to view challenges as opportunities for learning and personal development. It is the belief that our abilities and intelligence can be developed through dedication, hard work, and the willingness to embrace and learn from failure. When we adopt a growth mindset, we see setbacks as temporary setbacks rather than permanent roadblocks.

One of the key aspects of embracing a growth mindset is understanding that failure is not the end, but merely a stepping stone towards success. As entrepreneurs, we are bound to encounter setbacks and failures at some point in our journey. However, instead of allowing these failures to hinder our progress, we must harness their potential and extract valuable lessons from them.

Consider the story of Thomas Edison, the renowned inventor who famously said, "I have not failed. I've just found 10,000 ways that won't work." Edison's mindset exemplifies the power of embracing failure and turning it into an opportunity for growth. With each failed attempt, he learned valuable insights that propelled him closer to his eventual success.

To embrace a growth mindset, it is vital to celebrate effort and persistence rather than solely focusing on outcomes. Often, we tend to measure our success solely by the end result, overlooking the tremendous effort, dedication, and learning that goes into the process. However, it is during the process that we grow, develop new skills, and evolve as entrepreneurs.

By celebrating our efforts and acknowledging the steps we take towards overcoming obstacles, we fuel our motivation and drive. It becomes less about the immediate outcome and more about the continuous growth and improvement that we experience along the way. Embracing a growth mindset allows us to view challenges not as indicators of our limitations but as opportunities to expand our capabilities.

Moreover, when faced with challenges, a growth mindset encourages us to seek out feedback and guidance. Rather than perceiving feedback as criticism or a reflection of our inadequacy, we see it as a valuable source of insight and an opportunity for improvement. By actively seeking feedback from mentors, peers, and customers, we gain new perspectives, refine our strategies, and enhance our overall performance.

Additionally, cultivating a growth mindset requires us to intentionally step out of our comfort zones and embrace the unfamiliar. Many entrepreneurs tend to gravitate towards what feels safe and familiar. However, growth and innovation lie beyond the boundaries of comfort. When we challenge ourselves to explore new paths, take calculated risks, and venture into uncharted territories, we open doors to new opportunities and breakthroughs.

Moreover, a growth mindset enables us to reframe our mindset from a fixed mindset, where we believe our abilities are fixed and limited, to a growth mindset, where we recognize our capacity for growth and improvement. This shift in mindset allows us to view challenges not as daunting hurdles but as opportunities to learn, adapt, and reinvent ourselves.

As we immerse ourselves in the entrepreneurial journey, embracing a growth mindset becomes pivotal in navigating the unpredictable terrain filled with setbacks and hurdles. It allows us to transform challenges into stepping stones towards success, redefine our limitations, and continually strive for growth and achievement.

The journey towards cultivating a growth mindset requires commitment, resilience, and a genuine desire to learn and improve. Remember, the most significant growth often occurs outside of our comfort zones. Embrace the challenges, seek feedback, celebrate your efforts, and never shy away from failure. In doing so, you will unlock your full potential and discover the endless opportunities that await on the other side.

The journey towards embracing a growth mindset has only just begun. In the next part of this chapter, we will explore practical strategies and techniques to foster and sustain a growth mindset, enabling you to overcome any obstacle that crosses your path. Stay tuned as we delve deeper into the wonderful world of growth mindset and unlock its transformative power! In the first half of this chapter, we explored the importance of embracing a growth mindset as entrepreneurs. We discovered that challenges and obstacles are not roadblocks but rather opportunities for learning and personal development. Thomas Edison's story served as a powerful example of how failure can be transformed into a stepping stone towards success. We also discussed the significance of celebrating effort and persistence and seeking feedback and guidance. Additionally, we highlighted the need to step out of our comfort zones and view challenges as opportunities to learn, adapt, and reinvent ourselves.

As we continue on this journey of embracing a growth mindset, let us delve deeper into practical strategies and techniques that will help us foster and sustain this powerful mindset.

One essential aspect of cultivating a growth mindset is developing a strong sense of self-awareness. Taking the time to reflect on our strengths, weaknesses, and areas for improvement allows us to identify areas where growth is possible. A helpful tool in this process is journaling. By putting our thoughts and experiences onto paper, we gain clarity and insights that can drive personal growth. Journaling also enables us to track our progress and reinforce the belief in our ability to overcome challenges.

In addition to self-reflection, surrounding ourselves with like-minded individuals who support and encourage growth is paramount. Building a network of mentors, peers, and fellow entrepreneurs provides us with diverse perspectives and valuable guidance. Engaging in discussions, attending networking events, and seeking mentorship opportunities allows us to tap into a vast pool of knowledge and experiences. By learning from others who have faced similar challenges and achieved success, we can accelerate our growth and navigate obstacles more effectively.

Furthermore, embracing a growth mindset requires us to shift our focus from comparing ourselves to others to striving for personal improvement. It is natural to look at successful entrepreneurs and feel a sense of admiration or even envy. However, constantly comparing ourselves to others can hinder our progress and diminish our self-confidence. Instead, we should channel that energy towards self-improvement and focus on charting our unique path to success. Remember, every entrepreneur's journey is different, and it is the lessons we learn along the way that truly shape our success.

Moreover, as we cultivate a growth mindset, we must embrace the power of positive thinking. The way we perceive and interpret challenges greatly impacts our ability to overcome them. By reframing negative thoughts into positive affirmations, we can shift our mindset and approach challenges with optimism and resilience. For example, instead of thinking, "I can't do this," we can reframe it as, "I am capable of overcoming any obstacle that comes my way." This subtle shift in language and mindset can play a significant role in how we tackle challenges and ultimately achieve our goals.

An often overlooked yet incredibly vital aspect of embracing a growth mindset is taking care of our mental and physical well-being. The demanding nature of entrepreneurship can take a toll on our health, energy levels, and motivation. Therefore, it is crucial to prioritize self-care and create a healthy work-life balance. Engaging in activities that bring us joy, practicing mindfulness or meditation, and maintaining a healthy lifestyle all contribute to our overall well-being and enable us to face challenges with a clear and focused mind.

As we near the end of this chapter, I urge you to hold onto the belief that challenges are not barriers but opportunities for growth and success. Embracing a growth mindset empowers us to overcome obstacles with resilience, creativity, and a willingness to learn. It allows us to unleash our full potential, exceed our own expectations, and continually strive for personal and professional growth.

Remember, every challenge you encounter on your entrepreneurial journey is an invitation to grow and evolve. So, embrace the unknown, celebrate your progress, seek support and guidance when needed, and trust in your ability to navigate any obstacle that comes your way. With a growth mindset as your guiding force, there are no limits to what you can achieve.

Congratulations on making it through this chapter! In the next part of this book, we will dive into the practical application of a growth mindset in various aspects of the entrepreneurial journey. Get ready to embrace its transformative power and unlock a world of opportunities!

Chapter 3: Identifying Limiting Beliefs

Learn techniques for recognizing and challenging your limiting beliefs that hinder your ability to turn problems into opportunities.

In the journey towards success, entrepreneurs often encounter numerous challenges and obstacles. These obstacles can arise from external factors, such as market fluctuations or competitive pressures, but more often than not, the biggest barriers lie within ourselves. These barriers are our limiting beliefs – deeply ingrained thoughts and perceptions that hold us back from reaching our true potential.

Limiting beliefs act as an invisible prison, confining us to a narrow view of what we can achieve. They stem from past experiences, societal norms, or fear of failure. However, the key to converting problems into opportunities lies in identifying and challenging these self-imposed limitations.

The first step in this process is self-awareness. To conquer our limiting beliefs, we must become conscious of the thoughts and beliefs that shape our actions and decisions. Take a moment to reflect on your personal and professional life. Are there any recurring patterns that hinder your progress? Do you often find yourself hesitating or doubting your abilities when faced with a challenging situation? These may be indications of limiting beliefs.

One effective technique for uncovering these beliefs is journaling. Set aside some time each day to write down your thoughts and emotions regarding specific situations. Look for recurring themes or negative self-talk that may be holding you back. By externalizing your thoughts, you gain a fresh perspective and can identify patterns that limit your growth.

Another valuable tool for recognizing limiting beliefs is mindfulness. Practice being fully present in the moment and observe your thoughts without judgment. Notice any doubts, fears, or negative self-talk that arises and acknowledge them. By becoming aware of these thoughts, you can start to dismantle their power.

Once you've identified your limiting beliefs, it's essential to challenge them. Ask yourself whether these beliefs are serving your growth and progress or holding you back. Often, limiting beliefs are based on assumptions rather than facts. Question the evidence that supports these beliefs. Is it valid in your current context? Are there alternative perspectives or possibilities that challenge these beliefs?

Seeking diverse perspectives is instrumental when challenging limiting beliefs. Engage in conversations with trusted mentors, peers, or industry experts who can provide different outlooks on your challenges. They can help you question your assumptions and offer valuable insights that broaden your understanding.

To further challenge your limiting beliefs, seek out real-life examples of individuals who have overcome similar hurdles and achieved remarkable success. Reading biographies or case studies can be incredibly inspiring and uplifting. These stories serve as reminders that limitations are often self-imposed and that with determination and the right mindset, problems can indeed be transformed into opportunities.

As entrepreneurs, we are continually faced with adversity, setbacks, and unexpected challenges. Yet, by recognizing and challenging our limiting beliefs, we gain the power to shift our perspective and approach these hurdles with renewed courage and determination. Within every problem lies the seed of opportunity, waiting to be discovered by those who dare to challenge their own self-imposed limitations.

Remember, the first step towards converting problems into opportunities is self-awareness. Take the time to identify your limiting beliefs, challenge them, and seek alternative perspectives. By doing so, you pave the way for the second half of this chapter, where we will delve deeper into practical techniques to transform these challenges into catalysts for growth and success.

So, stay tuned for the next part of this chapter, where we'll share powerful strategies to harness your potential and give a 180-degree spin to your challenges. Exciting times lie ahead, and your entrepreneurial journey is about to take a transformative turn. As we delve deeper into the exploration of identifying and challenging limiting beliefs, we unlock the potential to transform challenges into catalysts for growth and success. In the first half of this chapter, we discovered the power of self-awareness and the techniques of journaling, mindfulness, seeking diverse perspectives, and gaining inspiration from real-life examples. Now, we will explore practical strategies to harness your potential and give a 180-degree spin to your challenges.

One effective technique to challenge limiting beliefs is reframing. Reframing involves looking at a situation from a different perspective, allowing you to shift your mindset towards a more positive and solution-oriented outlook. When faced with a challenge, ask yourself, "How can I view this situation differently? What opportunities can arise from this obstacle?" By reframing the problem, you open yourself up to innovative thinking and creative solutions that were previously hidden.

Another powerful strategy is goal-setting. By setting clear and achievable goals, you create a roadmap to success and focus your energy on productive actions. When setting goals, it is essential to envision the outcome you desire and align your beliefs with that vision. Break down your larger goals into smaller, manageable steps, and celebrate each milestone along the way. This approach not only keeps you motivated and on track but also challenges any limiting beliefs that may arise during the journey.

In addition to goal-setting, adopting a growth mindset is crucial for overcoming limiting beliefs. Embrace the belief that challenges are opportunities for learning and growth. Instead of viewing setbacks as failures, see them as valuable lessons that bring you closer to success. Embrace the idea that your abilities and intelligence are not fixed, but can be developed through dedication, effort, and a willingness to adapt. By embracing this mindset, you transform challenges into stepping stones towards personal and professional advancement.

As entrepreneurs, it is also vital to surround ourselves with a network of support. Seek out individuals who believe in your potential and can offer guidance and encouragement along the way. Connect with mentors who have overcome their own limiting beliefs and can provide valuable insights from their experiences. Join mastermind groups or entrepreneurial communities where you can share your challenges and gain wisdom from like-minded individuals. Remember, the power of collaboration and support can provide the necessary fuel to conquer your limiting beliefs and turn challenges into opportunities.

Furthermore, cultivating self-compassion is essential in the process of identifying and challenging limiting beliefs. When we encounter setbacks or face challenges, we often engage in harsh self-criticism that reinforces our limiting beliefs. Instead, practice self-compassion by treating yourself with kindness, understanding, and forgiveness. Acknowledge that failure is a natural part of the learning process and that it does not define your worth or potential. By showing yourself compassion, you break free from the grips of self-doubt and open yourself up to the transformative power of growth.

Lastly, take consistent action towards challenging your limiting beliefs. Knowledge alone is not enough; it is through action that we solidify our newfound awareness and create lasting change. Each day, commit yourself to take small steps outside of your comfort zone.

Challenge the beliefs that tell you what you cannot achieve or the limits you have imposed upon yourself. By consistently taking action and pushing your boundaries, you strengthen your resilience, expand your capabilities, and create new opportunities.

Remember, as entrepreneurs, you have the power to give a 180-degree spin to your challenges. By identifying and challenging your limiting beliefs, reframing your perspective, setting clear goals, adopting a growth mindset, seeking support, practicing self-compassion, and taking consistent action, you will unleash your full potential and pave the way for success.

In conclusion, you have already taken the crucial first step of self-awareness in identifying your limiting beliefs. Now, armed with the practical strategies provided in this chapter, it is time to put those beliefs to the test. The transformational journey you are about to embark on will undoubtedly be filled with ups and downs, but it is within these challenges that the seeds of opportunity reside. Embrace the power within you, challenge your self-imposed limitations, and unleash your true potential to convert problems into remarkable opportunities. Exciting times lie ahead, and remember, you have the ability to create your own success story.

Chapter 4: Embracing Failure as a Stepping Stone

Failure. It's a word that often carries a heavy burden, one that entrepreneurs know all too well. We live in a society that tends to view failure as a source of shame and disappointment. It's time to challenge this perception and reframe failure as an essential part of the entrepreneurial journey - a stepping stone towards growth and success.

For entrepreneurs, failure should no longer be seen as a negative outcome but rather as a valuable learning experience. It is through failure that we gain valuable insights, develop resilience, and refine our strategies. Every successful entrepreneur has faced setbacks and obstacles along the way, but it is their ability to embrace failure that sets them apart and propels them forward.

One of the key reasons why failure is crucial to an entrepreneur's journey is that it provides invaluable feedback. When things don't go according to plan, it offers an opportunity to reflect and evaluate what went wrong. By analyzing failures, entrepreneurs can identify areas for improvement, uncover hidden weaknesses, and refine their approach. This feedback loop is a powerful tool for personal and professional growth.

Embracing failure also nurtures resilience. As an entrepreneur, you will inevitably face challenges that test your determination and drive. Each failure serves as a test of your character, pushing you to persist and adapt. It is in these moments of failure that you discover your true strength and develop the resilience needed to withstand future obstacles. Remember, success is not about avoiding failure altogether but rather bouncing back stronger when faced with adversity.

Moreover, failure opens doors to new possibilities and opportunities. It forces us to step out of our comfort zones and explore alternative paths. When one door closes, another opens, and it is often through failure that we stumble upon unexpected breakthroughs. Many of the greatest inventions and innovations have emerged from initial failures or setbacks. Embracing failure allows us to seize these hidden opportunities and turn them into catalysts for success.

Another important aspect of failure is its role in building empathy and humility. Failure humbles us and reminds us that we are not infallible. It teaches us to be empathetic towards others who face their own challenges and failures. By acknowledging our own shortcomings and vulnerabilities, we become better leaders and collaborators. Failure fosters a sense of humility that is vital in building meaningful relationships, both in business and in life.

As entrepreneurs, it is essential to shift our mindset and see failure not as an end, but as a necessary part of the journey. The path to success is not a straight line; it is a winding road filled with twists and turns. Each failure brings us closer to our goals, helping us refine our strategies and guiding us towards success. By embracing failure, we cultivate resilience, gain invaluable feedback, discover unexpected opportunities, and nurture humility and empathy.

In the next part of this chapter, we will delve deeper into the practical ways entrepreneurs can effectively embrace failure and transform it into a powerful tool for growth. We will explore strategies to navigate through failure, cultivate resilience, and extract valuable lessons from setbacks. Prepare yourself for practical insights and actionable steps that will equip you to embrace failure as a stepping stone on your entrepreneurial journey. Stay tuned for the surprising yet transformational second half of this chapter. In the previous section, we explored the importance of embracing failure as a valuable stepping stone on the entrepreneurial journey. We discussed how failure provides crucial feedback, nurtures resilience, opens doors to new opportunities, and fosters empathy and humility. Now, let us delve deeper into practical ways entrepreneurs can effectively embrace failure and transform it into a powerful tool for growth.

1. Learn from Mistakes:

When faced with failure, it is imperative to take a step back and analyze the situation objectively. Identify the areas that contributed to the failure and critically assess your own decision-making process. By pinpointing the specific mistakes made, you can learn valuable lessons and make adjustments for future endeavors. Remember, failure is not about assigning blame, but about understanding how to improve.

2. Adapt and Pivot:

One of the key traits of successful entrepreneurs is their ability to adapt and pivot in the face of failure. When a particular approach or strategy proves unsuccessful, it is essential to be flexible and willing to make necessary changes. This could involve tweaking your business model, exploring new markets, or even completely pivoting your product or service. Embracing failure allows for innovation and exploration of alternative paths to success.

3. Surround Yourself with Support:

Failure can be emotionally challenging, and it is crucial to have a strong support system in place. Surround yourself with mentors, fellow entrepreneurs, or a trusted network who can provide guidance, wisdom, and encouragement during tough times. Remember, you are not alone in your experiences, and seeking support from others who have faced and overcome failure can provide valuable insights and motivation.

4. Reframe Failure as a Positive Opportunity:

As entrepreneurs, reframing failure as a positive opportunity is essential. Instead of viewing failure as a setback, see it as an opportunity for growth and improvement. Embrace the mindset that every failure brings you closer to success by providing valuable lessons and insights that will refine your entrepreneurial journey. Remember, successful entrepreneurs have encountered numerous failures along the way, and it is their ability to learn from them that sets them apart.

5. Develop Resilience:

Resilience is the ability to bounce back from failure and persevere through challenges. It is the fuel that keeps entrepreneurs going when faced with adversity. To develop resilience, focus on building a growth mindset and maintaining a positive attitude. Embrace challenges as learning opportunities and see setbacks as temporary roadblocks rather than permanent failures. It is through resilience that you can harness the power of failure and transform it into a catalyst for success.

6. Celebrate Small Wins:

Amidst failure, it is essential to acknowledge and celebrate small wins along the way. Recognize the progress made, even if it may seem insignificant compared to your ultimate goals. By celebrating small victories, you can maintain motivation, boost morale, and reinforce the belief that failure is not a definitive outcome but rather a stepping stone towards success. Remember, Rome wasn't built in a day, and success is often the result of continuous effort and relentless determination.

In conclusion, failure is not the end of the road for entrepreneurs. It is a necessary part of the journey that propels growth, creativity, and resilience. By embracing failure, learning from mistakes, adapting to new circumstances, seeking support, and reframing failure as a positive opportunity, entrepreneurs can effectively navigate through setbacks and transform them into powerful tools for growth. Cultivating resilience and celebrating small victories along the way are key ingredients to turning failure into success. So, dear entrepreneurs, embrace failure with open arms and let it guide you towards the extraordinary possibilities that lie beyond. The entrepreneurial journey is filled with promise and potential, and by embracing failure as a stepping stone, there is no limit to what you can achieve.

Chapter 5: Developing Resilience and Adaptability

In the ever-evolving world of entrepreneurship, challenges and uncertainties are ubiquitous. As entrepreneurs, we are constantly confronted with hurdles that can either break us or make us stronger. How we navigate through these obstacles and respond to change is crucial for our personal growth and the success of our ventures. It is in these moments that resilience and adaptability become vital traits to cultivate.

Resilience, often likened to the ability to bounce back, is the inner strength that allows us to withstand adversity and persevere. It is the power that enables us to confront setbacks head-on, learn from our experiences, and thrive amidst uncertainty. Resilient entrepreneurs have a tenacious spirit that propels them forward, giving them the courage and determination to overcome obstacles.

So, how can we develop resilience? It begins with a mindset shift – embracing challenges as opportunities for growth rather than setbacks. Reflecting on past experiences, we can examine how we handled difficulties and extract valuable lessons for future encounters. It is in these moments of self-reflection that we realize the power lies within us to redefine our perception and response to challenges.

Another key aspect of cultivating resilience is building a support network. Surrounding ourselves with like-minded individuals who understand the entrepreneurial journey can provide valuable emotional and practical support. Through shared experiences and empathetic listening, we can find solace, advice, and inspiration. Collaborating with others who have faced similar challenges can often lead to innovative solutions and a renewed sense of determination.

Additionally, practicing self-care plays an integral role in developing resilience. As entrepreneurs, we tend to prioritize our ventures above all else, often neglecting our own well-being in the process. However, true resilience stems from nourishing our minds, bodies, and spirits. Taking time for rest, exercise, and hobbies can rejuvenate our energy and build emotional resilience.

Adaptability, the ability to adjust and thrive in the face of change, complements resilience. In the fast-paced world of entrepreneurship, change is inevitable. Markets shift, technologies evolve, and consumer preferences change rapidly. Entrepreneurs who embrace adaptability possess the agility to respond quickly and effectively to these changes.

To cultivate adaptability, we must first become comfortable with uncertainty. Rather than resisting change, we must view it as an opportunity for growth and innovation. This requires developing a mindset that is open to new possibilities and willing to take calculated risks. By constantly seeking knowledge and staying updated on industry trends, we can position ourselves to adapt swiftly to changing circumstances.

Embracing a growth mindset is another crucial aspect of adaptability. Seeing failures and setbacks as stepping stones rather than roadblocks allows us to continuously learn and evolve. Entrepreneurs who maintain a growth mindset see challenges as opportunities for improvement, enabling them to adapt their strategies and find creative solutions.

Moreover, expanding our comfort zones and seeking diverse perspectives can enhance our adaptability. By actively seeking out new experiences and surrounding ourselves with individuals from different backgrounds and industries, we expose ourselves to fresh ideas and insights. This diversity of thought helps us develop a broader perspective, fostering adaptability in our approach to problem-solving.

To be a successful entrepreneur, resilience and adaptability are like two sides of the same coin. They complement each other, helping us navigate through the inevitable ups and downs of the entrepreneurial journey. By building resilience and cultivating adaptability, we not only overcome challenges but also discover new possibilities and opportunities that lie hidden within them.

With an unwavering spirit and the willingness to adapt, we can overcome any obstacle that comes our way. Challenges transform into catalysts for growth, and uncertainty becomes the breeding ground for innovation. As entrepreneurs, we have the power to harness these traits and thrive amidst the ever-changing landscape of entrepreneurship. The second half of this chapter will delve deeper into practical strategies to further develop resilience and adaptability, equipping you with the tools needed to navigate the entrepreneurial world with confidence and tenacity. Stay tuned for the journey ahead. Developing resilience and adaptability as an entrepreneur is an ongoing process that requires continuous learning and growth. In the second half of this chapter, we will delve deeper into practical strategies that will further equip you with the tools needed to navigate the entrepreneurial world with confidence and tenacity.

One effective strategy to enhance resilience and adaptability is to embrace a problem-solving mindset. As entrepreneurs, we encounter numerous challenges on a daily basis. Instead of viewing these challenges as roadblocks, we should approach them as opportunities for problem-solving and innovation. By reframing our mindset and adopting a "can-do" attitude, we empower ourselves to find creative solutions and adapt swiftly to changing circumstances.

To develop this problem-solving mindset, it is crucial to seek out diverse perspectives. Surrounding ourselves with individuals from different backgrounds and industries allows us to tap into a wealth of ideas and insights. Collaborating with people who think differently from us can spark fresh perspectives and pave the way for innovative problem-solving. Encourage open dialogues and actively listen to the opinions and experiences of others. This diversity of thought will help you think outside the box and adapt your strategies effectively.

Another practical strategy to enhance resilience and adaptability is to be proactive in seeking knowledge and staying updated on industry trends. The world is constantly evolving, and as entrepreneurs, we must stay ahead of the curve. Dedicate time every day to research industry news, attend conferences, and engage in networking events. By staying informed and aware of emerging trends, we position ourselves to adapt swiftly to changes in the market or consumer preferences.

Simultaneously, it is essential to maintain a growth mindset. View failures and setbacks not as defeats, but as opportunities for growth and learning. Embrace the mindset that setbacks are temporary and can be overcome with perseverance and tenacity. Learn from your mistakes, adjust your strategies, and move forward. Entrepreneurs who maintain a growth mindset are not afraid to take risks and are constantly seeking ways to improve and grow.

Building a solid support network is also crucial for developing resilience and adaptability. Surround yourself with like-minded individuals who understand the entrepreneurial journey and can offer emotional and practical support. Engage in mastermind groups, where entrepreneurs can share experiences, brainstorm innovative solutions, and provide support during challenging times. Lean on your support network whenever you need guidance or encouragement.

Additionally, practicing self-care remains an integral part of developing resilience and adaptability. As entrepreneurs, it is easy to neglect our own well-being while prioritizing our ventures. However, true resilience stems from nourishing our minds, bodies, and spirits. Set aside time for rest, exercise, and engage in activities that bring you joy. Taking care of yourself allows you to approach challenges with a clear perspective and renewed energy.

In conclusion, developing resilience and adaptability as entrepreneurs is critical for success in the ever-changing landscape of entrepreneurship. By embracing a problem-solving mindset, seeking diverse perspectives, staying updated on industry trends, maintaining a growth mindset, and building a strong support network, you can enhance your ability to thrive amidst challenges and uncertainty.

Remember that challenges are not roadblocks but stepping stones towards growth and innovation. With the right mindset and tools, you have the power to transform obstacles into opportunities. Embrace the journey of entrepreneurship with an unwavering spirit and the willingness to adapt. Resilience and adaptability are not just traits to possess but a way of life for successful entrepreneurs. Keep pushing forward, and may your entrepreneurial journey be filled with boundless possibilities and triumphs.

Chapter 6: Finding Opportunities in Market Trends

In the fast-paced world of business, entrepreneurs must constantly keep their finger on the pulse of the market. The ability to spot emerging trends and seize the opportunities they present is what sets successful entrepreneurs apart from the rest. Market trends, whether they are societal changes, technological advancements, or shifts in consumer preferences, hold immense potential for transforming problems into profitable business ventures. In this chapter, we will explore the art of recognizing market trends and leveraging them to your advantage.

To begin, it is crucial to stay informed about current events and consumer behaviors. By reading industry publications, attending conferences, and engaging in networking events, entrepreneurs can gain valuable insights into the ever-evolving market landscape. Stay curious, be proactive, and maintain an open mind as you navigate through the vast sea of information.

One effective approach to spotting emerging market trends is to identify patterns and connect the dots. Analyze data from various sources, such as market research reports, customer surveys, and online forums. Look for commonalities and subtle shifts that may indicate a potential trend. For example, if you notice a rising demand for eco-friendly packaging across different industries, it could signify a growing consumer preference for sustainable products. By recognizing this trend early on, you can position yourself to cater to this emerging market and gain a competitive edge.

Another valuable tool for trend-spotting is social media. Platforms like Twitter, Instagram, and Facebook offer a treasure trove of real-time information. Monitor conversations, hashtags, and influencers relevant to your industry. Look for topics gaining traction and garnering attention. By tapping into these online conversations, you can gauge customer sentiment and identify potential opportunities.

Moreover, never underestimate the power of observation and intuition. Sometimes, the most significant trends reveal themselves in everyday life. Pay attention to the world around you, from the latest fashion fads to advancements in technology. Ask yourself how these changes could impact consumer behavior and create new business possibilities. Trust your gut instincts and allow yourself to think outside the box.

Once you have identified a market trend, the next step is to leverage it effectively. This involves adapting your business strategy to align with the emerging opportunities. Look for ways to incorporate the trend into your products, services, or marketing efforts. This might mean redesigning your packaging to be environmentally friendly or developing software that caters to the changing needs of remote workers. The key is to evolve alongside the trend while staying true to your core values and unique selling proposition.

Furthermore, collaboration can be a powerful tool in harnessing market trends. Seek out partnerships with like-minded entrepreneurs or other businesses that complement your offerings. By combining resources and expertise, you can create innovative solutions that cater to the demands generated by the trend. Collaborations not only amplify your potential impact but also provide valuable networking opportunities and expand your customer base.

In conclusion, spotting and capitalizing on emerging market trends is a vital skill for entrepreneurs. By staying informed, analyzing data, and relying on intuition, you can identify promising opportunities. Leveraging these trends requires adaptability, creativity, and collaboration. As the business landscape continues to evolve, entrepreneurs who embrace change and transform challenges into opportunities will thrive. Will you be one of them? Stay tuned for the second half of this chapter where we will dive deeper into strategies for leveraging market trends to unlock your entrepreneurial potential. With our newfound knowledge of identifying market trends, let's now delve into how we can effectively leverage these opportunities to transform problems into successful business ventures. As an entrepreneur, adaptability, creativity, and collaboration will be key in staying ahead of the curve.

Once you have identified a market trend, it is crucial to evaluate how it aligns with your business goals and values. Take the time to assess the potential impact and feasibility of incorporating this trend into your products, services, or marketing efforts. Consider how you can adapt your existing offerings to cater to the changing needs and preferences of your target audience.

One effective strategy is to redesign your products or services to reflect the emerging trend. For example, if you have noticed an increased demand for eco-friendly packaging, you can explore sustainable alternatives and integrate them into your operations. Whether it's using recyclable materials or embracing innovative packaging designs, this adaptation can demonstrate your commitment to sustainability while capturing the attention of environmentally-conscious consumers.

Another way to leverage market trends is by developing new products or services that directly cater to the emerging demands. Analyze the market landscape and identify any gaps or unmet needs that the trend presents. By filling these gaps, you can position your business as a pioneer and leader in the industry. For instance, if remote work is becoming more prevalent, you may consider developing software tools or services specifically designed to enhance productivity and collaboration for remote teams.

Furthermore, collaboration can be a powerful tool in leveraging market trends. Seek out partnerships with likeminded entrepreneurs or businesses that complement your offerings. By combining resources, expertise, and unique perspectives, you can create innovative solutions that address the demands generated by the trend. Collaborations not only amplify your potential impact but also provide valuable networking opportunities and expand your customer base. Together, you can capitalize on the market trend and mutually benefit from each other's strengths.

In addition to collaboration, leveraging the power of marketing and branding is essential in capitalizing on market trends. Craft compelling messages and narratives that resonate with your target audience's aspirations and values. Showcase how your business is uniquely positioned to address their evolving needs and desires. By effectively communicating your commitment to the trend, you can attract and retain customers who share the same values, creating a loyal customer base.

Moreover, don't overlook the importance of continuous innovation. As market trends evolve, it is vital to stay ahead of the curve and consistently innovate your offerings. Keep a finger on the pulse of the market, staying attuned to emerging changes and consumer preferences. This may require conducting regular market research, engaging with your target audience, and monitoring competitors' strategies. By staying proactive and responsive, you can adapt your business to meet evolving customer demands, ensuring your continued success.

Lastly, never underestimate the power of agility and the ability to pivot when necessary. While leveraging market trends can bring immense opportunities, it is essential to remain flexible and adaptable. As circumstances change, be prepared to reassess and adjust your strategies accordingly. The ability to pivot and embrace new trends as they emerge will allow you to maintain your entrepreneurial edge and sustain long-term growth.

In conclusion, by effectively leveraging market trends, entrepreneurs can transform problems into profitable business opportunities. Through adaptation, creativity, collaboration, and continuous innovation, you can position your business at the forefront of emerging trends and attract a loyal customer base. Remember, the key lies in recognizing these trends, aligning them with your business goals, and seizing the opportunities they present. As an entrepreneur, the ability to navigate the ever-evolving business landscape will be crucial for your long-term success. Embrace change, think entrepreneurially, and unlock your full potential by making market trends work for you. Your journey to success starts now.

Chapter 7: Leveraging Technology for Innovation

In today's rapidly evolving business landscape, success often hinges on the ability to adapt and embrace technological advancements. Technology has revolutionized the way we live, work, and interact with the world around us. For entrepreneurs, leveraging these advancements can provide a unique opportunity to innovate and tackle challenges head-on. In this chapter, we will explore how embracing technology can help entrepreneurs turn challenges into competitive advantages, opening doors to new possibilities and propelling their ventures to new heights.

Technology has the power to disrupt industries, transform business models, and create new markets. As an entrepreneur, it is crucial to stay ahead of the curve and recognize the potential of technology as a catalyst for innovation. By harnessing the power of technological tools and solutions, entrepreneurs can address their challenges creatively and find novel ways to stand out in the competitive marketplace.

One key aspect of leveraging technology for innovation is automation. Automation has become increasingly prevalent across various industries, streamlining processes and reducing human error. From manufacturing to customer service, entrepreneurs can automate repetitive tasks, enabling them to focus on higher-value activities that drive growth and creativity. With automation, entrepreneurs can improve efficiency, minimize costs, and allocate their resources more strategically, giving them a competitive edge in the market.

Another area where technology offers immense potential for innovation is data analytics. In today's digital age, vast amounts of data are generated every second. By harnessing the power of advanced analytics tools, entrepreneurs can gain valuable insights into consumer behavior, market trends, and operational efficiencies. These insights can inform strategic decision-making, enabling entrepreneurs to better understand their customers, identify untapped opportunities, and tailor their offerings to meet evolving demands. Data analytics empowers entrepreneurs to make data-driven decisions, mitigating risks and maximizing the probability of success.

Cloud computing is yet another technological advancement that presents unparalleled opportunities for entrepreneurs. The ability to store, access, and analyze data on remote servers offers scalability, flexibility, and cost-efficiency. With cloud computing, entrepreneurs can leverage powerful computing resources without investing in expensive hardware infrastructure. This allows them to focus on their core business activities and rapidly adapt to changing market dynamics. Additionally, cloud-based collaboration tools enable entrepreneurs to collaborate seamlessly with team members and stakeholders, regardless of geographical boundaries. This fosters innovation, creativity, and agility, empowering entrepreneurs to embrace globally distributed talent and work collaboratively to solve complex challenges.

Emerging technologies such as artificial intelligence (AI), machine learning, and the Internet of Things (IoT) are also poised to revolutionize entrepreneurship. AI-powered algorithms can automate decision-making processes, optimize resource allocation, and enhance customer experiences. Machine learning algorithms can analyze vast datasets to identify patterns, make predictions, and drive innovation. The IoT connects devices and systems, enabling entrepreneurs to gather real-time data, automate processes, and create interconnected ecosystems. These technologies provide entrepreneurs with unprecedented opportunities to innovate, differentiate themselves, and create unique value propositions in the market.

As we delve further into the second half of this chapter, we will explore specific examples and success stories of entrepreneurs who have successfully leveraged technology for innovation. Through their experiences, we will uncover strategies and best practices that can guide aspiring entrepreneurs on their own journey to convert problems into opportunities.

Stay tuned as we navigate the exciting world of technological advancements and innovation. In the next part of this chapter, we will dive deeper into practical steps entrepreneurs can take to leverage technology and explore how this transforms challenges into competitive advantages. Trust that by embracing technology, entrepreneurs can unlock their potential, embrace change, and thrive in today's dynamic business landscape. There is no limit to what can be achieved when technology and entrepreneurship join forces - together, they hold the key to unlocking a world of innovation and endless possibilities. With our understanding of the power of technology in driving innovation and turning challenges into competitive advantages, let us now delve deeper into practical steps that entrepreneurs can take to leverage technology effectively.

One of the key steps is to identify the specific pain points or challenges within your business. Technology can be a powerful tool, but it needs to be applied strategically. By pinpointing the areas that require improvement or optimization, you can direct your resources towards finding the right technological solutions. This targeted approach ensures that your investment in technology is purposeful and aligned with your business goals.

Once you have identified your pain points, the next step is to research and explore the technological solutions available. The ever-evolving landscape of technology introduces new possibilities and tools regularly. It is crucial to stay informed about the latest developments and cutting-edge innovations in your industry. This knowledge will help you make informed decisions and choose the technologies that best suit your business needs.

The implementation of technology requires careful planning to ensure a smooth transition. It is essential to assess your existing infrastructure and determine if any upgrades or modifications are necessary. Furthermore, you should consider the compatibility and integration of new technologies with your current systems. Seamless integration enhances efficiency and minimizes disruption, enabling you to maximize the benefits of technology.

Collaboration is another key aspect to consider when leveraging technology for innovation. Engaging with experts, industry leaders, and technology providers can provide valuable insights and guidance. Building partnerships and fostering collaborations with technology-driven companies can help entrepreneurs access knowledge and expertise that they may not possess in-house. By tapping into external resources, entrepreneurs can accelerate their learning curve and gain a competitive edge in their respective markets.

To ensure a successful integration of technology, entrepreneurs should also prioritize staff training and development. It is essential to equip your team with the necessary skills and knowledge to utilize new technologies effectively. Providing training programs and resources enables your employees to embrace innovation and empowers them to become active contributors to your business growth.

As entrepreneurs embark on their journey of leveraging technology, it is vital to regularly measure and evaluate the impact of these technological advancements. Implementing performance metrics, data analytics, and key performance indicators (KPIs) allows you to monitor the effectiveness of the technologies implemented. This data-driven approach enables you to make informed decisions, refine your strategies, and optimize your use of technology over time.

Throughout this chapter, we have explored the transformative potential of various technological advancements for entrepreneurs. Automation streamlines processes, data analytics provides valuable insights, cloud computing offers scalability and flexibility, and emerging technologies like AI, machine learning, and IoT drive innovation. The possibilities are vast, and the opportunities for entrepreneurs are endless.

Technology has the ability to revolutionize your business, but it is crucial to remember that it is not a magic solution. It is a tool that requires strategic vision, careful planning, and continuous adaptation. Embracing technology is an ongoing process, and as entrepreneurs, it is essential to remain agile and open-minded to new possibilities.

As we conclude this chapter on leveraging technology for innovation, let us reflect on the remarkable journey we have embarked on. We have explored the immense power of technology in helping entrepreneurs turn challenges into competitive advantages. By embracing technology, entrepreneurs have the opportunity to unlock their potential, adapt to change, and thrive in today's dynamic business landscape.

Remember, the path to success may be filled with obstacles, but with technology as their ally, entrepreneurs have the means to navigate through them and transform them into stepping stones towards growth and success. So, embrace technology, embrace innovation, and embrace the endless possibilities that lie ahead. The future is yours to shape, and technology is your greatest ally. Go forth, entrepreneurs, and conquer new heights!

Chapter 8: Building a Supportive Network

In the journey of entrepreneurship, it is easy to underestimate the power of a supportive network. As you face challenges and navigate through uncharted territories, having a circle of like-minded individuals can make all the difference. Surrounding yourself with people who understand your aspirations, share your vision, and provide support, insights, and inspiration can be the catalyst that propels you forward during challenging times.

When we think about building a supportive network, the first question that comes to mind is, "Who should be part of this network?" The answer may vary depending on your specific goals, but there are a few fundamental traits to look for in your potential allies.

Seek out individuals who share your passion and ambition. These like-minded individuals understand the drive and determination required to pursue your entrepreneurial dreams. Whether they are fellow entrepreneurs, mentors, or industry experts, connecting with people who have a similar hunger for success can create a harmonious synergy that ignites your motivation to overcome obstacles.

It is equally crucial to surround yourself with individuals who possess complementary skills and knowledge. No one person can possess all the skills and expertise needed to tackle the diverse challenges of entrepreneurship. By forming alliances with individuals who excel in areas where you might lack, you can leverage their knowledge and expertise to find innovative solutions and accelerate your growth.

When building your supportive network, remember that the diversity of perspectives can be invaluable. Seek out individuals from different backgrounds and industries, as they can offer fresh insights and alternative approaches to problem-solving. Embrace the power of collaboration and leverage the collective wisdom of your network to expand your horizons and unlock new possibilities.

Supportive networks can take many forms, from formal mentorship programs to informal gatherings of like-minded individuals. Engaging in industry events, conferences, and workshops can be a fertile ground for networking opportunities. Attend relevant seminars and participate in panel discussions to meet individuals who can add value to your entrepreneurial journey.

In addition, online platforms and social media have revolutionized the way we connect with others. Utilize these platforms to establish meaningful relationships with individuals who share your entrepreneurial spirit. Engage in online groups, forums, and communities that are relevant to your niche, where you can interact with like-minded entrepreneurs, exchange ideas, and offer support.

Another critical aspect of building a supportive network is nurturing meaningful relationships with your peers. It's easy to become so focused on one's own challenges and aspirations that we overlook the power of camaraderie. Don't hesitate to reach out to fellow entrepreneurs and offer support when they need it. Celebrate their victories, offer a listening ear during their struggles, and be the cheerleader they need. By fostering an environment of collaboration rather than competition, you create a network of individuals who are invested in each other's success.

Surrounding yourself with a supportive network serves as a source of inspiration during challenging times. It is in these moments of doubt and uncertainty that your network can offer encouragement, reminding you of your capabilities and reigniting your determination.

Together, you can remind each other of the bigger picture, the reason why you embarked on this entrepreneurial journey in the first place.

As you build your supportive network, remember that it is not merely about what you can gain but also what you can contribute. Be a source of inspiration and support for others, offering a helping hand when needed and sharing your own insights and experiences. The true power of a supportive network lies in the collective growth and empowerment of its members.

In conclusion, building a supportive network is crucial for entrepreneurs. Surrounding yourself with like-minded individuals who share your passion, possess complementary skills, and offer diverse perspectives can be transformative. They can provide the support, insights, and inspiration needed to navigate through challenges and seize opportunities. So, take the time to intentionally connect with individuals who can uplift you on this entrepreneurial journey.

When you build a supportive network, it becomes a sanctuary, a safe space where you can freely discuss your challenges and seek guidance from individuals who understand your journey. In the second half of this chapter, we will delve deeper into the practical strategies you can employ to cultivate and nurture this valuable network.

One of the most effective ways to connect with like-minded individuals is by actively participating in entrepreneurial communities and organizations. These groups create opportunities for you to engage with fellow entrepreneurs, share experiences, and learn from one another. Join local business associations, attend networking events, and seek out industry-specific organizations that align with your interests and goals.

In these communities, take the initiative to introduce yourself and engage in conversations. Share your own experiences, challenges, and successes openly, as this creates an environment of trust and authenticity. Remember, every entrepreneur has faced obstacles and setbacks along the way—by being vulnerable and opening up, you encourage others to do the same. Through these interactions, you can establish meaningful connections that may blossom into long-lasting friendships and partnerships.

Another way to expand your supportive network is by seeking out mentors or coaches who can guide you through your entrepreneurial journey. Mentors are experienced individuals who can offer valuable insights and advice based on their own experiences. They can provide you with a fresh perspective, challenge your assumptions, and help you navigate through difficult decisions.

When looking for a mentor, seek someone who has a genuine interest in your success and shares your values and vision. Look for individuals who have achieved what you aspire to achieve and are willing to invest their time and wisdom in helping you grow. Remember that mentorship is a two-way street, and you should be prepared to give as much as you receive. Offer your time, skills, and knowledge in return, as this will foster a stronger and more mutually beneficial relationship.

In addition to mentors, peer groups and mastermind circles can be incredibly beneficial for entrepreneurs. These groups consist of individuals who are at a similar stage of their entrepreneurial journey and meet regularly to provide support, share insights, and hold each other accountable. Being part of a peer group not only allows you to receive valuable feedback and guidance but also enables you to contribute your own expertise and perspective to help others.

Online platforms and social media communities also provide an incredible opportunity to connect with like-minded individuals. Participate in relevant online groups and communities, where you can interact with entrepreneurs from different regions and industries. Engage in discussions, share your thoughts, and ask for advice when needed. These platforms offer a vast pool of knowledge and experiences that can enrich your own entrepreneurial endeavors.

Once you have established relationships within your supportive network, be proactive in maintaining and nurturing them. Show genuine interest in the lives and businesses of your network members, regularly checking in on their progress and offering support or advice whenever necessary. Set aside time to meet up with them for coffee or virtual hangouts, fostering a sense of camaraderie and solidarity.

Remember that building a supportive network is not just about what you can gain but also about what you can contribute. Be a source of inspiration, offer your expertise, and celebrate the achievements of others within your network. By fostering an environment of collaboration and collective growth, you create a powerful ecosystem of entrepreneurs working together towards success.

In conclusion, building and maintaining a supportive network is an essential aspect of entrepreneurial success. Surrounding yourself with like-minded individuals, mentors, and peer groups provides the support, insights, and inspiration needed to overcome challenges and seize opportunities. Actively seek out opportunities to connect, share your experiences, and nurture relationships within this network. Together, as a collective force, you can transform obstacles into opportunities and achieve greater heights on your entrepreneurial journey. So, go ahead and embrace the power of collaboration, because by doing so, you are not just changing your own life but also contributing to the growth and success of others in your network.

Chapter 9: Harnessing Creativity to Solve Problems

Unlock your creative potential and learn how to approach problems from unconventional perspectives to find unique solutions.

In the quest for success, entrepreneurs often encounter various challenges that test their determination and problem-solving abilities. It is in these moments that creativity becomes a valuable asset, allowing us to think outside the box and transform problems into opportunities.

Creativity is not a luxury reserved for artists or inventors; it is a skill that can be honed and developed by anyone willing to embrace it. By harnessing creativity, we can reframe our approach to problem-solving and discover innovative solutions that propel us forward.

The first step in unlocking your creative potential is to foster an open mindset. Embrace curiosity and approach problems with a sense of wonder. A closed mind limits your ability to see alternative perspectives and hampers your creative thinking. Instead, be open to new ideas and be willing to consider possibilities beyond the conventional.

One powerful technique for embracing creativity is reframing challenges. Instead of viewing problems as roadblocks, see them as opportunities for growth. By reframing the problem, you can shift your perspective and uncover hidden potential. Remember, some of the greatest successes have emerged from seemingly insurmountable obstacles.

Another way to tap into your creativity is to explore different domains of knowledge. Sometimes, the most innovative ideas come from unexpected sources. Expand your horizons by reading books or exploring subjects that are outside of your comfort zone. By broadening your knowledge base, you can draw inspiration from diverse areas and apply fresh perspectives to problem-solving.

Collaboration is another essential aspect of harnessing creativity. Engaging with others who possess different expertise and viewpoints can unlock novel ideas and lead to groundbreaking solutions. Surround yourself with a network of individuals who inspire and challenge you. Together, you can pool your collective creativity and generate innovative approaches to problem-solving.

Embracing failure is a critical component of the creative process. When facing challenges, it is natural to encounter setbacks and roadblocks. However, rather than viewing failure as a defeat, see it as an opportunity to learn and grow. Adopt a growth mindset that sees failure as an integral part of the journey towards success. Embrace the lessons learned from your failures, and let them fuel your determination to find alternative paths to success.

As entrepreneurs, we often face constraints and limitations in our endeavors. Yet, creativity thrives within boundaries. Instead of being hindered by limitations, use them as catalysts for innovation. Constraints force us to think creatively and come up with inventive solutions. By reframing constraints as opportunities, we can unleash our imaginations and discover unique approaches to problem-solving.

Now that we have explored various strategies to unlock your creative potential, it's time to put these ideas into action. In the second half of this chapter, we will delve into specific techniques and exercises to enhance your creative thinking skills. We will explore brainstorming methods, mind mapping, and other tools that can help you overcome challenges and generate innovative solutions. Get ready to unleash your inner creativity and embark on a journey of problem-solving like never before.

Remember, creativity is a boundless resource that lies within each of us. By embracing it and adopting a fresh perspective, you can transform even the most daunting problems into exciting opportunities. So, stay curious, think outside the box, and let your creative spirit guide you towards newfound success. The journey to harnessing your creativity has just begun, and the possibilities that await you are infinite.

Embracing different perspectives and thinking outside the box is just the beginning of harnessing your creative potential as an entrepreneur. In the second half of this chapter, we will explore specific techniques and exercises that can further enhance your creative thinking skills. These tools will help you overcome challenges and generate innovative solutions like never before.

One of the most powerful tools in your creative toolkit is brainstorming. This technique allows you to generate a plethora of ideas in a short amount of time. When brainstorming, it's important to create a judgment-free zone where all ideas are welcomed. Encourage yourself and others to think freely and explore even the most unconventional concepts. Remember, in brainstorming, quantity matters more than quality. You can always refine and narrow down the ideas later.

To make the most of your brainstorming sessions, try incorporating mind mapping into your process. Mind maps are visual representations of ideas that allow you to see the connections between different concepts. Start by writing down the main problem or challenge at the center of a page and then branch out with various potential solutions or approaches. This technique helps you organize your thoughts and uncover new connections that may lead to breakthrough solutions.

Another effective technique for enhancing your creativity is "The Five Whys." This method involves asking "why" multiple times to uncover the root cause of a problem or challenge. By repeatedly digging deeper and questioning the initial answer, you can uncover hidden complexities and gain deeper insights. The Five Whys technique helps you move beyond surface-level solutions and encourages a more thorough understanding of the problem at hand.

As entrepreneurs, it's also important to rely on your network and engage in collaborative problem-solving. Surround yourself with individuals who possess diverse expertise and viewpoints. By working together, you can tap into each other's creativity and come up with groundbreaking solutions. Collaboration not only expands your perspectives but also fosters a sense of camaraderie and support that can invigorate your problem-solving efforts.

In addition to collaboration, seeking inspiration from other industries or domains can fuel your creativity. Take the time to explore books, articles, or documentaries that are outside of your comfort zone. Look for parallels or lessons that can be applied to your own challenges. Sometimes, the most innovative ideas come from unexpected sources, and by broadening your knowledge base, you'll be better equipped to find unique solutions.

As you continue on your journey of problem-solving, remember to embrace failure with a growth mindset. Setbacks and roadblocks are inevitable, but they provide valuable learning opportunities. Each failure brings you one step closer to success. Analyze what went wrong, adapt your approach, and try again. Failure is not the end; it's merely a stepping stone on your path towards finding the right solution.

Lastly, to truly unlock your creative potential, integrate playfulness into your problem-solving process. Play stimulates the imagination, encourages risk-taking, and removes the fear of failure. Create an environment that promotes playful exploration and experimentation. Encourage yourself and those around you to take imaginative leaps and think outside the confines of what is expected. Remember, some of the most successful innovations have emerged from playful experimentation.

As entrepreneurs, you have the power to convert problems into opportunities through harnessing your creativity. By embracing open-mindedness, reframing challenges, seeking collaboration, and incorporating various techniques like brainstorming, mind mapping, and the Five Whys, you can overcome obstacles and discover solutions that are truly unprecedented. Remember, the possibilities that await you are infinite, so stay curious, think creatively, and let your entrepreneurial spirit soar. Unleash your inner creativity and prepare for a journey of problem-solving unlike anything you've experienced before.

Chapter 10: Cultivating a Positive Mindset

Discover the power of positivity and how it can transform challenges into opportunities through a shift in mindset.

In the fast-paced world of entrepreneurship, it's easy to get caught up in the whirlwind of daily challenges. From dealing with tight deadlines to navigating through uncertain markets, entrepreneurs often find themselves facing a multitude of obstacles. However, what sets successful entrepreneurs apart is their ability to cultivate a positive mindset, which enables them to view these challenges as stepping stones towards growth and success.

A positive mindset is not about ignoring or denying the existence of problems. It's about consciously choosing to react to challenges in a way that empowers us rather than disempowers us. Instead of allowing frustration and negativity to take over, successful entrepreneurs train themselves to see problems as opportunities in disguise.

One of the key aspects of cultivating a positive mindset is reframing. It's about shifting our perspective and looking at challenges from a different angle. By doing so, we can uncover hidden opportunities that may have otherwise been overlooked. For example, let's imagine you're launching a new product and unexpectedly encounter a production delay. Instead of viewing this as a setback, a positive mindset allows you to see it as an opportunity to refine your product or explore alternative marketing strategies. Seeing obstacles as opportunities fuels creativity and innovation, ultimately propelling the entrepreneur toward success.

Moreover, a positive mindset brings mental and emotional benefits that extend beyond problem-solving. Research has shown that maintaining an optimistic outlook has numerous health benefits and can lead to increased resilience, better coping mechanisms, and improved overall well-being. As an entrepreneur, your mental and emotional state greatly influences your ability to lead and inspire others. By cultivating a positive mindset, not only are you more equipped to navigate challenges, but you also create a ripple effect within your team, fostering a positive and supportive work environment.

To begin cultivating a positive mindset, it's essential to practice self-awareness. Pay attention to your thoughts and emotions when faced with challenges. Are you prone to react with frustration and despair, or do you see an opportunity for growth? Recognizing your default mindset in challenging situations is the first step towards consciously choosing a positive perspective. With time and practice, you can rewire your brain to default to a positive mindset, even in the face of adversity.

Another powerful tool in developing a positive mindset is the practice of gratitude. Expressing gratitude not only helps shift your focus from problems to blessings but also enhances your ability to find the silver lining in difficult situations. Consider keeping a gratitude journal and writing down three things you are grateful for each day. This simple practice can have a profound impact on your overall outlook and mindset.

In addition to reframing challenges and practicing gratitude, surrounding yourself with positive influences is crucial. Seek out mentors, attend networking events, and engage with a community of like-minded entrepreneurs who share your passion and optimism. The power of collective positive energy is unparalleled.

As we conclude the first half of this chapter, dear entrepreneur, remember that cultivating a positive mindset is an ongoing journey.

It takes time and effort to rewire your thinking patterns and develop resilience in the face of challenges. However, by embracing the power of positivity, you unlock limitless possibilities, transforming obstacles into opportunities and paving the way for entrepreneurial success.

And with that, we leave you with the notion that a positive mindset holds the key to unlocking the full potential within you. In the second half of this chapter, we delve deeper into actionable strategies and mindset shifts that will help you harness the power of positivity in your entrepreneurial journey. Stay tuned for the thrilling revelations that await you and be prepared to witness the remarkable transformations that lie ahead. The adventure continues...As we continue on this journey of cultivating a positive mindset, dear entrepreneur, let us dive deeper into actionable strategies and mindset shifts that will empower you to harness the power of positivity in your entrepreneurial journey.

One powerful tool for cultivating a positive mindset is the practice of visualization. Visualization involves creating a vivid mental image of your desired outcome. By visualizing success and envisioning yourself overcoming challenges, you train your mind to focus on positive possibilities rather than dwelling on obstacles. Visualization helps you develop a clear sense of direction and instills confidence in your ability to navigate any difficulties that come your way.

Take a moment to close your eyes and imagine your business thriving, flourishing amidst any obstacles. Picture yourself confidently tackling challenges, finding innovative solutions, and achieving your goals. Allow yourself to feel the satisfaction and joy that comes from turning problems into opportunities. Visualization not only helps you cultivate a positive mindset, but it also fuels motivation and inspires action towards your desired outcomes.

Another essential aspect of cultivating a positive mindset is practicing self-compassion. As entrepreneurs, we can be incredibly hard on ourselves, especially when faced with setbacks or failures. However, berating ourselves only feeds negativity and undermines our ability to bounce back. Instead, practice self-compassion by treating yourself with kindness, understanding, and forgiveness.

When encountering challenges, remind yourself that setbacks are a natural part of the entrepreneurial journey. Recognize that mistakes and failures provide valuable learning experiences that propel you towards growth and improvement. Embrace the idea that every problem is an opportunity for personal and professional development. By showing yourself compassion and reframing setbacks as stepping stones, you foster resilience and foster a more positive mindset.

In addition to visualization and self-compassion, the language we use plays a pivotal role in shaping our mindset. The words we choose can either uplift us or weigh us down. Therefore, it is essential to replace negative and limiting language with positive and empowering alternatives.

For instance, instead of saying, "I can't do this," reframe your statement to, "I am capable of finding a solution." By making this simple shift in language, you shift your perspective and empower yourself to take on challenges. Language has the power to influence our thoughts, emotions, and actions, so let's choose our words wisely and consciously.

Building a support system of like-minded individuals is also crucial to cultivating a positive mindset. Surrounding yourself with optimistic, ambitious, and supportive individuals can provide the encouragement and inspiration needed during challenging times. Seek out networking events, join entrepreneurial groups, or engage in online communities where you can connect with fellow entrepreneurs who share your passion and optimism. Together, you can uplift and motivate one another, continuously fueling each other's positive energy.

Lastly, an effective practice in cultivating a positive mindset is setting aside time for relaxation, reflection, and self-care. In the busy world of entrepreneurship, it can be easy to neglect our mental and emotional well-being. However, incorporating activities that bring you joy and peace allows you to recharge and maintain a positive mindset.

Whether it's engaging in hobbies, spending quality time with loved ones, practicing mindfulness or meditation, or simply taking a walk-in nature, these moments of self-care replenish your energy and provide the clarity needed to navigate challenges with a positive mindset. Remember, taking care of yourself is not a luxury; it is essential to your success as an entrepreneur.

As we come to the end of this chapter, my dear entrepreneur, I invite you to embrace the power of positivity. Cultivating a positive mindset is not only about transforming challenges into opportunities; it is about transforming yourself. You have the ability to rewrite the narrative, to see obstacles as stepping stones, and to create a remarkable entrepreneurial journey filled with growth, resilience, and success.

Remember, as you cultivate a positive mindset, you inspire those around you and create a ripple effect in your team and beyond. Your unwavering optimism and entrepreneurial spirit become a guiding light for others, fostering a positive and supportive work environment.

So, go forth with confidence and determination, dear entrepreneur. Embrace the power of positivity, and unlock the full potential within you. The adventure continues, and the possibilities are limitless.

Chapter 11: Turning Setbacks into Comebacks

Learn strategies to bounce back from setbacks stronger than ever, using them as stepping stones towards success.

Setbacks. We've all experienced them at some point in our lives, both personally and professionally. As entrepreneurs, setbacks are inevitable. They can range from a minor hiccup to a major roadblock. The key to success lies in how we handle these setbacks and, more importantly, how we can turn them into opportunities for growth and advancement.

It's natural to feel discouraged when faced with a setback. You may question your abilities, doubt your decisions, or fear failure. However, it's important to remember that setbacks are not permanent. They are temporary obstacles that can be overcome with the right mindset and strategies. In fact, setbacks can provide valuable lessons and insights that can propel us forward.

The first step in turning setbacks into comebacks is to shift our perspective. Instead of viewing setbacks as failures, we should see them as opportunities for learning and growth. Every setback is a chance to reassess our approach and make necessary adjustments. It's important to embrace the belief that setbacks are not a reflection of our abilities or potential, but rather stepping stones towards success.

One powerful strategy for bouncing back from setbacks is to cultivate resilience. Resilience is the ability to adapt and bounce back from adversity. It's about developing a mindset that sees challenges as opportunities for growth. Resilient entrepreneurs understand that setbacks are an inherent part of the journey and use them as fuel to propel themselves forward.

To cultivate resilience, it's important to practice self-care. Take time to recharge, both physically and mentally. Surround yourself with a support system of like-minded individuals who can provide guidance and encouragement. Build a network of mentors who have experienced setbacks themselves and can offer valuable insights. Remember, you don't have to face setbacks alone.

Another effective strategy is to analyze setbacks objectively. Take a step back and evaluate the situation. What went wrong? What can be learned from this setback? This analysis will help you identify areas for improvement and develop strategies to prevent similar setbacks in the future. It's important to approach setbacks with a growth mindset, embracing them as opportunities for learning and improvement.

In addition, setbacks can provide a unique opportunity to pivot and explore new possibilities. Sometimes, setbacks push us out of our comfort zones and force us to consider alternative paths. Embracing change and being open to new opportunities can lead to unexpected successes. Remember, some of the most successful businesses today have emerged from unexpected setbacks and pivots.

Moreover, setbacks can also serve as a reality check. They remind us to stay humble and focused on our goals. Setbacks can reveal weaknesses or blind spots that we may have overlooked in our pursuit of success. By acknowledging and addressing these weaknesses, we can fortify our foundations and strengthen our future endeavors.

To truly turn setbacks into comebacks, it's important to maintain a positive attitude and a vision for the future. See setbacks as temporary detours on the road to success, rather than permanent roadblocks. Embrace the belief that every setback brings you one step closer to your ultimate destination.

In conclusion, setbacks are an inevitable part of the entrepreneurial journey. They test our resilience, challenge our abilities, and push us to grow. But with the right mindset and strategies, setbacks can be transformed into opportunities for learning, growth, and even greater success. As entrepreneurs, let's embrace setbacks, learn from them, and come back stronger than ever. The second half of this chapter will delve deeper into specific strategies and examples to help you maximize the potential of setbacks as stepping stones towards success. Stay tuned.

Now that we have explored the importance of shifting our perspective and cultivating resilience when faced with setbacks, let's delve deeper into specific strategies and examples that will help you bounce back stronger than ever. These strategies have been employed by successful entrepreneurs who have turned setbacks into opportunities for growth and advancement.

One powerful strategy is to practice goal-setting and focus. It's crucial to establish clear and ambitious goals that align with your vision for success. By setting specific targets, you create a roadmap that keeps you motivated and focused, even in the face of setbacks. Goals act as beacons of light, guiding you through challenging times. When setbacks arise, reassess your goals and determine if any adjustments are necessary. This adaptability ensures that setbacks don't derail your progress but rather serve as catalysts for reevaluation and improvement.

Another key element to consider is maintaining a growth mindset. Successful entrepreneurs understand that setbacks are not personal failures but rather opportunities for learning and improvement. Embrace the belief that there is always room for growth and that setbacks are stepping stones towards your ultimate destination. By fostering a growth mindset, you will continually seek new knowledge, develop new skills, and remain adaptable in the face of challenges. Remember, it is through adversity that we truly grow and evolve.

In addition to a growth mindset, building a strong support system is paramount. Surround yourself with like-minded individuals who understand the entrepreneurial journey and can provide guidance, encouragement, and a fresh perspective during setbacks. Mentorship is invaluable during challenging times, as mentors have experienced setbacks themselves and can offer valuable insights and advice. By nurturing relationships with mentors and peers, you gain access to a network of support that will enable you to bounce back stronger and wiser.

Adaptability is another critical factor in turning setbacks into comebacks. Setbacks often reveal areas where you can pivot and explore new possibilities. Sometimes, the path you initially set out on may not be the most effective, and setbacks force you to consider alternative approaches. Embrace change, be open to new opportunities, and be willing to adjust your strategies accordingly. By adapting to new circumstances, you may discover innovative solutions and unexpected successes that would not have been possible without setbacks.

Moreover, setbacks offer valuable learning experiences that can shape your future decisions and actions. Every setback provides an opportunity for self-reflection and analysis. Take the time to evaluate what went wrong and identify areas for improvement. By objectively analyzing setbacks, you gain invaluable insights that can help prevent similar setbacks in the future. Remember, setbacks are not random occurrences but rather signposts that guide you towards success.

Lastly, it's crucial to maintain a positive attitude and vision for the future. Setbacks can be demoralizing, but it is essential to remember that they are temporary detours, not permanent roadblocks. Cultivate optimism and resilience, and remind yourself of your ultimate goals. Embrace setbacks as learning opportunities that bring you one step closer to success. By maintaining a positive mindset, you create space for innovation, creativity, and determination to thrive, enabling you to rise above setbacks and achieve your entrepreneurial vision.

In conclusion, setbacks are an integral part of the entrepreneurial journey. Entrepreneurs who embrace setbacks as opportunities for growth understand that setbacks are not permanent but rather temporary obstacles that can be overcome with the right mindset and strategies. Through shifting our perspective, cultivating resilience, practicing goal-setting, maintaining a growth mindset, building a support system, adapting to new circumstances, and learning from setbacks, we can turn setbacks into comebacks. Remember, setbacks are not the end of the road but rather stepping stones towards the success you envision. Stay resilient, remain focused on your goals, and continue to defy odds. With the strategies and examples discussed in this chapter, you can transform setbacks into opportunities and come back stronger than ever before.

Stay tuned for more valuable insights and strategies.)

Chapter 12: Embracing Change as an Entrepreneur

Change is the only constant in life, and as an entrepreneur, it lies at the very heart of your journey. The path you have chosen demands that you become comfortable with the idea of change and learn to embrace it wholeheartedly. The ability to navigate change effectively is not only crucial for your own growth but is also key to the success and sustainability of your entrepreneurial ventures.

Change can take many forms in the world of entrepreneurship. It could be a shift in the market landscape, advancements in technology, evolving customer preferences, or even internal factors such as team dynamics or business strategy. Regardless of its source, change presents you with both challenges and opportunities.

One of the first steps to embracing change is to understand why it holds such significance in the realm of entrepreneurial growth. Change acts as a catalyst for progress, innovation, and improvement. It pushes you out of your comfort zone, forcing you to continually adapt and evolve. It presents you with new perspectives and fresh ideas, enabling you to discover unexplored avenues for success.

Change also allows you to discover hidden opportunities. As an entrepreneur, you must learn to see beyond the initial turbulence that change often brings. While others may view change as disruptive or intimidating, you have the ability to perceive it as a gateway to innovation and growth. By embracing change, you position yourself to uncover valuable insights and capitalize on emerging trends, giving you a competitive edge in the market.

Navigating change effectively requires a proactive and strategic mindset. It begins with a willingness to embrace uncertainty and let go of the fear of the unknown. Rather than resisting change, successful entrepreneurs learn to view it as an invitation for transformation and progress. They understand that change is not a sign of failure or weakness but rather an opportunity to create something extraordinary.

To navigate change effectively, it is vital to develop a few key skills. First and foremost, you must cultivate adaptability. This means being open to new ideas, being flexible in your thinking, and being willing to pivot when circumstances require it. As an entrepreneur, your ability to adapt quickly can mean the difference between success and failure in a rapidly changing marketplace.

Another critical skill in navigating change is resilience. As an entrepreneur, you will undoubtedly face setbacks and obstacles along the way. It is during these moments of challenge that your resilience will be put to the test. Resilience allows you to bounce back from failure, learn from your mistakes, and use adversity as a stepping stone towards growth.

Effective communication is also essential when embracing change. As an entrepreneur, you must effectively convey your vision and objectives to your team and stakeholders. Clear and open communication fosters a sense of unity, trust, and shared purpose, making it easier to navigate change collectively. By keeping everyone informed and engaged, you set the stage for collaborative problem-solving and innovation.

As we venture further into the realm of embracing change as an entrepreneur, we will explore strategies to leverage change as an opportunity rather than a burden. From harnessing the power of a growth mindset to capitalizing on disruptive trends, this chapter aims to equip you with the tools and insights you need to embrace change with open arms.

Remember, the entrepreneurial journey is not just about building successful businesses, but also about personal and professional growth. Embracing change and navigating it effectively are vital components of this journey. By understanding the importance of change, developing key skills, and adopting a proactive mindset, you position yourself for long-term success and create a legacy of innovation and resilience.

Now that we've explored the significance of embracing change as an entrepreneur, we're ready to dive deeper into the strategies and practices that will help you navigate change efficiently and transform challenges into opportunities. In the second half of this chapter, we will delve into practical tips, real-life examples, and actionable insights that will empower you to thrive in the dynamic world of entrepreneurship. So, get ready to embark on a journey of discovery and transformation as we unlock the secrets of embracing change as an entrepreneur. Stay tuned for the next part of this chapter, where we unravel the tools, you need to master the art of navigating change! In the dynamic world of entrepreneurship, embracing change is not just a choice, but a necessity. As we navigate through the trials and triumphs of this journey, it becomes evident that change holds the key to unlocking our fullest potential and achieving long-term success. In the second half of this chapter, we will dive into practical strategies and actionable insights that will empower you to thrive in the face of change.

One essential aspect of embracing change is cultivating a growth mindset. The entrepreneurial landscape is constantly evolving, and to stay ahead, we must embrace a mindset of continuous learning and improvement. A growth mindset allows us to see challenges as opportunities for growth and development, rather than roadblocks. It enables us to approach change with curiosity, resilience, and a willingness to step outside our comfort zones. By fostering a growth mindset, we can transform obstacles into stepping stones and create new possibilities for ourselves and our ventures.

Another vital tool in navigating change is staying informed and adaptable. The world around us is changing at an unprecedented pace, driven by advancements in technology, shifts in consumer behavior, and evolving market trends. As entrepreneurs, we must stay abreast of these changes and adapt our strategies accordingly. This requires a willingness to continuously acquire new knowledge, seek out emerging trends, and pivot our approaches when needed. By staying adaptable, we can position ourselves to leverage change as a catalyst for innovation and growth.

Furthermore, forming strategic partnerships and building a strong support network can greatly enhance our ability to navigate change. As entrepreneurs, we often face complex challenges that require diverse expertise and perspectives. Surrounding ourselves with individuals who share our vision and values can provide us with valuable insights, guidance, and support during times of change. These collaborations can foster resilience, enhance problem-solving abilities, and amplify our impact in the marketplace. By harnessing the power of collective intelligence, we can transform change into a collaborative endeavor that drives us towards success.

In the face of change, it is crucial to maintain a sense of purpose and clarity of vision. As entrepreneurs, our ventures are built on a strong foundation of passion and purpose. When confronted with change, it is essential to revisit our core values and mission. By anchoring ourselves in our purpose, we can remain steady amidst uncertainty and make strategic decisions that align with our long-term goals. This sense of purpose not only guides us through change but also inspires and motivates our team, creating a shared sense of resilience and commitment.

Lastly, self-care and resilience are paramount when navigating change. The entrepreneurial journey can be demanding and challenging, and change often brings added stress and pressure. Taking care of our mental, emotional, and physical well-being is crucial for maintaining resilience in the face of change. Prioritizing self-care practices such as exercise, meditation, and seeking support from trusted mentors or coaches can help us build the resilience needed to adapt, bounce back, and thrive in the ever-changing entrepreneurial landscape.

As we reach the end of this chapter, it is clear that embracing change is not a one-time event or a fleeting concept; it is a mindset and a way of life for entrepreneurs. By proactively embracing change, maintaining a growth mindset, staying adaptable, fostering strong partnerships, staying aligned with our purpose, and prioritizing self-care, we equip ourselves with the tools and insights needed to navigate change effectively.

Remember, change is not something to be feared or avoided, but rather an opportunity for transformation and progress. By embracing change, we position ourselves to not only overcome challenges but also uncover untapped potential and create extraordinary outcomes. As entrepreneurs, we have the power to give a 180-degree spin to our challenges and convert them into opportunities for growth, innovation, and resilience.

So, as you embark on your entrepreneurial journey, embrace change with open arms, and let it be the fuel that propels you towards greatness. Stay tuned for the next chapter, where we will delve deeper into other aspects of entrepreneurship that will support your growth and success. Until then, keep embracing change, stay adaptable, and continue to shape the world with your entrepreneurial spirit.

Chapter 13: Identifying Market Gaps and Unmet Needs

In the ever-evolving world of entrepreneurship, the key to success lies in the ability to identify and harness market gaps and unmet needs. These gaps represent untapped potential waiting to be explored and turned into profitable business opportunities. As an entrepreneur, it is crucial to possess the vision and mindset that allows you to see beyond challenges, turning them into stepping stones towards success.

Identifying market gaps and unmet needs is not as daunting as it may seem. In fact, it starts with a simple question: "What problems can I solve?" By diving into this question and exploring various industries and sectors, you open up a world of possibilities. Successful entrepreneurs have a unique ability to identify gaps in the market and turn them into innovative solutions. Take Steve Jobs, for example, he recognized the need for a user-friendly personal computer and transformed the entire technology industry with the creation of Apple.

To identify market gaps, you must first become an insightful observer. Pay close attention to the needs and frustrations of consumers and businesses around you. Start by conducting thorough market research and gathering relevant data. This will provide you with valuable insights into what is missing or lacking in the current market. By staying informed and analyzing trends, you can uncover hidden opportunities waiting to be seized.

Another effective technique in identifying market gaps is by engaging in conversations and actively listening to your target audience. Entrepreneurs who establish genuine connections with their customers are better positioned to uncover unmet needs. Attend industry events, participate in social media communities, or conduct surveys to gain a deeper understanding of the challenges faced by your potential customers. By empathizing with their pain points, you lay the foundation for creating valuable solutions.

Collaboration is another powerful tool in identifying market gaps and unmet needs. Networking and engaging with professionals in various fields can provide a fresh perspective on existing markets. Interacting with like-minded individuals who share your passion for entrepreneurship can lead to vital insights and innovative ideas. Remember, the entrepreneurial journey is not one that should be traveled alone. Together, we can address market gaps and create a positive impact.

Beyond observation and collaboration, it is crucial to stay curious and open-minded. Embrace the mindset of constant learning and growth. By staying updated on industry trends and technological advancements, you equip yourself with the knowledge to spot emerging market gaps. Explore different sectors, attend workshops, and engage in continuous education. The more you invest in expanding your horizons, the greater the opportunities you can uncover.

Now, armed with the knowledge of how to identify market gaps and unmet needs, it's time to take action. Entrepreneurship thrives on turning challenges into opportunities. As you venture into the business world, remember that obstacles are not roadblocks but stepping stones towards success. Embrace the mindset that every problem carries within it the seed of opportunity. It is through this perspective that you can transform market gaps and unmet needs into thriving business ventures.

The second part of this chapter will delve deeper into the strategies and tactics needed to capitalize on these identified market gaps. Brace yourself for an exploration into innovation, resourcefulness, and the art of seizing opportunities. Together, we will unlock the doors to success as we learn how to give a 180-degree spin to our challenges.

Now that we have set the foundation for identifying market gaps and unmet needs, let your mind wander and anticipate the surprises that lay ahead. Are you ready to take the next step on our entrepreneurial journey? Prepare yourself for the possibilities that await us in the second half of this chapter.

Remember, the power lies within you to convert problems into opportunities. Stay tuned for the continuation of this enlightening chapter as we delve deeper into the art of transforming market gaps into thriving businesses. Your next adventure awaits! As we embark on the second half of this enlightening chapter, let us delve deeper into the strategies and tactics required to capitalize on the market gaps and unmet needs that we have identified. Brace yourself for an exploration into innovation, resourcefulness, and the art of seizing opportunities. Together, we will unlock the doors to success as we learn how to give a 180-degree spin to our challenges.

Now that we have set the foundation for identifying market gaps and unmet needs, it is time to let your mind wander and anticipate the surprises that lie ahead. Are you ready to take the next step on our entrepreneurial journey? Prepare yourself for the possibilities that await us.

One of the key strategies to convert market gaps into thriving businesses is to innovate. Innovation is the lifeblood of entrepreneurship, and it allows us to create unique solutions that address the unmet needs of our target audience. Embrace a mindset of constant improvement and strive to think outside the box.

To foster innovation, encourage creativity within your team and establish an environment that promotes free thinking. Encourage brainstorming sessions, where ideas flow freely and no idea is considered too far-fetched. Remember, some of the greatest inventions and breakthroughs stemmed from seemingly crazy ideas.

Additionally, resourcefulness is a crucial skill in turning market gaps into opportunities. As entrepreneurs, we often face limited resources and constraints. However, resourcefulness allows us to make the most of what we have and find creative solutions to overcome obstacles.

Think about how you can leverage your existing resources, whether it is your network, skills, or knowledge. Look for alternative ways to achieve your goals and consider unconventional strategies. Resourcefulness often leads to innovative approaches that set you apart from the competition and enable you to provide unique value to your customers.

Another important aspect of seizing market gaps is to understand your target audience deeply. Dive into their lives, their aspirations, and their pain points. What are their desires and frustrations? By empathizing with your customers, you can identify their unmet needs and develop solutions that truly resonate with them.

Market research plays a crucial role in understanding your target audience. Conduct surveys, collect feedback, and analyze data to gain valuable insights into their preferences and behaviors. Use these insights to refine your products or services, ensuring that they solve the exact problems your customers face.

Furthermore, stay attuned to industry trends and technological advancements. Adaptability is key in the ever-evolving business landscape. By keeping up with the latest developments, you can spot emerging market gaps and position yourself as an early mover.

Attend industry conferences, read industry publications, and engage with thought leaders in your field. Embrace continuous learning and be open to new ideas. The more you immerse yourself in your industry, the better equipped you will be to identify and seize opportunities as they arise.

Lastly, remember that the entrepreneurial journey is not meant to be traveled alone. Seek out mentors, advisors, and like-minded individuals who share your passion and enthusiasm for entrepreneurship. Networking not only expands your knowledge but also opens doors to potential collaborations and partnerships.

Surround yourself with people who challenge and inspire you, who can offer different perspectives and insights. Collaboration allows us to combine our strengths and leverage the collective wisdom of a diverse group. Together, we can address market gaps and create a positive impact.

As we conclude this chapter on identifying market gaps and unmet needs, I hope you feel empowered to turn challenges into opportunities. Remember, obstacles are not roadblocks but stepping stones towards success. It is through the lens of possibility that we can transform market gaps into thriving business ventures.

By embracing innovation, resourcefulness, and a deep understanding of our target audience, we can position ourselves for success. Keep your entrepreneurial spirit alive and continue to seek opportunities for growth and learning.

Congratulations on completing this chapter! Take a moment to reflect on the insights you have gained and the strategies you have learned. Let them fuel your entrepreneurial journey, as you venture into the unknown and seize the unlimited potential that lies within market gaps and unmet needs.

Stay tuned for the rest of this book as we explore more aspects of converting problems into opportunities. Each chapter builds on the previous one, equipping you with valuable tools and insights to succeed as an entrepreneur.

Remember, as entrepreneurs, we have the power to shape the world around us. Embrace the challenges, embrace the opportunities, and embrace the extraordinary journey that lies ahead.

Chapter 14: Overcoming Fear and Taking Calculated Risks

Fear has a way of paralyzing us, making our dreams feel out of reach and our goals seem unattainable. It lurks in the shadows, whispering doubts and insecurities into our minds. But what if I told you that fear could be harnessed? What if, instead of letting it hold you back, you could use it as a catalyst for growth and innovation? In this chapter, we will explore strategies for overcoming fear, embracing risk, and unleashing your true potential as an entrepreneur.

Fear is a natural response to the unknown. It's what keeps us rooted in our comfort zones, where we feel safe and secure. But growth and success lie just beyond those boundaries. It's time to step out of the familiar and embrace the possibilities that lie before you. As an entrepreneur, taking risks is part of your journey. It's how you pave the way for innovation and create new opportunities.

One effective strategy for overcoming fear is to confront it head-on. Take a moment to identify what exactly you are afraid of. Is it failure? Rejection? The unknown? By understanding the root cause of your fear, you can begin to address it directly. Break it down into smaller, more manageable pieces and tackle them one by one. Remember, courage is not the absence of fear, but the ability to act in spite of it.

Another way to overcome fear is through preparation and knowledge. Educate yourself about the risks involved in your ventures. Research, study, and learn from those who have gone before you. This will equip you with the tools and confidence to make informed decisions rather than succumbing to fear-driven hesitation. Taking calculated risks means weighing the potential outcomes and rewards, and being willing to accept the consequences, positive or negative.

Embracing a growth mindset is crucial when it comes to overcoming fear and taking risks. Understand that failure is not a setback; it's an opportunity to learn and grow. The most successful entrepreneurs have faced countless failures along their journey but have used them as stepping stones to success. Shift your perspective and view failures as valuable learning experiences that propel you forward.

Surround yourself with a supportive network of like-minded individuals who encourage and inspire you. Seek out mentors who have weathered their own storms and come out stronger on the other side. Their guidance and wisdom can help you navigate the challenging terrain of risk-taking with more confidence and clarity. Remember, you don't have to face your fears alone. Lean on those who believe in you and your potential.

As an entrepreneur, your ability to embrace risk and overcome fear will directly impact your level of innovation. Fear stifles creativity and limits your ability to think outside the box. When you dare to take risks, you open the floodgates of innovation and invite new ideas to flow freely. Embrace the discomfort that comes with venturing into uncharted territory, for it is in these moments that groundbreaking ideas are born.

The first half of this chapter has explored strategies for overcoming fear, embracing risk, and using it as a catalyst for growth and innovation. We have seen how confronting fear, preparing through knowledge, cultivating a growth mindset, and building a supportive network can empower entrepreneurs to take calculated risks and push the boundaries of what is possible.

But this is only the beginning. The second half of this chapter will delve even deeper into the realm of risk-taking and uncover the secrets to transforming challenges into opportunities. So, stay tuned for the continuation, where we will unlock the hidden potential that lies within your fears and discover how taking calculated risks can lead to unprecedented growth and success. Overcoming Fear and Taking Calculated Risks: Part Two

Now that we have explored strategies for overcoming fear and embracing risk in the first half of this chapter, it is time to delve even deeper into the realm of risk-taking and uncover the hidden potential that lies within your fears.

As an entrepreneur, you are well aware that challenges and obstacles are a natural part of the journey. But instead of seeing them as roadblocks, we can choose to see them as opportunities for growth and success. This shift in perspective is key to converting problems into opportunities.

To truly embrace risk, it is vital to develop resilience and the ability to bounce back from failure. The most successful entrepreneurs understand that setbacks are not permanent, but temporary moments of redirection. By learning from failures and continually adapting, you can turn setbacks into stepping stones towards your goals.

One powerful technique to overcome fear is visualization. Take a moment to imagine yourself successfully navigating through the risks and challenges that lie ahead. Create a mental picture of the outcome you desire. Embrace the feelings of accomplishment and the joy of overcoming your fears. By visualizing your success, you are programming your mind to believe in your abilities and to stay focused on achieving your goals.

Another essential aspect of risk-taking is trusting your instincts. As an entrepreneur, you have the advantage of being driven by passion and intuition. While it is essential to gather knowledge and expertise, sometimes the best opportunities arise when you follow your gut feelings. Trust yourself and your ability to make sound decisions, even in the face of uncertainty.

Furthermore, it is crucial to maintain a positive mindset throughout your journey. Cultivate self-belief and surround yourself with positivity. Celebrate small victories along the way, recognizing that each step forward is progress. Remember, success is not always a linear path. It consists of peaks and valleys, and the most successful entrepreneurs have experienced both. Embrace the highs and lows, for they are the tapestry of your entrepreneurial journey.

As you face risks head-on, it is important to manage your expectations. Not every risk will lead to immediate success, and that's okay. Embrace the process and trust that each experience is a valuable lesson. Adaptability and flexibility will be your greatest assets as you navigate through the ever-changing landscape of entrepreneurship.

Additionally, it is beneficial to seek constructive feedback to refine your approach. Connect with mentors, advisors, and fellow entrepreneurs who can provide valuable insights and fresh perspectives. Actively seek out opportunities to learn from those who have traveled a similar path. Their wisdom and guidance will help you make informed decisions and refine your risk-taking strategies.

Above all, remember that taking calculated risks is not just about achieving success; it is about personal growth and continuous learning. Embrace a growth mindset and cherish the experiences that arise from facing your fears. With each risk you take, you are expanding your comfort zone and allowing for new opportunities to emerge.

In conclusion, fear and risk-taking are interconnected elements of the entrepreneurial journey. By confronting fear head-on, preparing through knowledge, cultivating a growth mindset, building a supportive network, visualizing success, trusting your instincts, maintaining a positive mindset, managing expectations, and seeking feedback, you have the power to convert challenges into opportunities.

As you continue on your path as an entrepreneur, remember that you are not alone. The challenges you face are shared by countless others who have walked similar paths. Embrace the unknown, step out of your comfort zone, and let your fears fuel your growth and innovation.

Congratulations on taking the first steps towards embracing risk and converting problems into opportunities. In the face of fear, you have shown courage and determination. So go forth, fellow entrepreneur, and may your journey be filled with remarkable achievements and endless possibilities.

Chapter 15: Reframing Problems as Challenges

Learn the art of reframing problems as challenges, allowing you to approach them with a proactive and solution-oriented mindset.

In our entrepreneurial journey, we often encounter obstacles and setbacks that can lead us to feel overwhelmed and discouraged. These problems can be like dark clouds overshadowing our path, obstructing our progress. However, by mastering the skill of reframing, we can transform these problems into opportunities, turning our challenges into stepping stones on the road to success.

The first step in reframing problems as challenges is to cultivate a positive mindset. Instead of viewing problems as insurmountable roadblocks, see them as opportunities for growth and development. Embrace the belief that every problem carries within it the potential for innovation and improvement. By shifting our perspective, we open ourselves up to a world of possibilities.

Next, it is essential to analyze the problem from different angles. Take a step back and examine the situation objectively. What factors contributed to this problem? Are there any hidden opportunities concealed within it? By dissecting the problem, we gain a deeper understanding of its root causes and can identify potential solutions.

One effective way to reframe problems as challenges is by asking ourselves empowering questions. Instead of dwelling on what went wrong, ask yourself, "What can I learn from this situation?" or "How can I turn this setback into an opportunity?" These questions shift our focus from the problem itself to the potential solutions and lessons it holds. They inspire us to find creative ways to overcome the challenge at hand.

Another valuable tool in reframing problems is visualization. Close your eyes and imagine yourself triumphing over the obstacle. Picture yourself confidently navigating through the challenge, emerging on the other side stronger and more resilient. By visualizing success, you send powerful messages to your subconscious mind, priming yourself for victory.

Furthermore, embrace the mindset of experimentation. Treat problems as experiments, opportunities to test different strategies and approaches. Understand that failure is not a setback but an essential part of the learning process. The path to success is rarely linear, and through trial and error, we discover innovative solutions that propel us forward. Embrace the uncertainty and embrace the opportunity to learn and grow.

In addition, surround yourself with a supportive network. Connect with fellow entrepreneurs who have faced similar challenges and learn from their experiences. Seek guidance and advice from mentors who have successfully reframed their own problems and turned them into opportunities. By building a strong support system, you gain access to valuable insights and encouragement, helping you stay on track even during the most challenging times.

Remember, reframing problems as challenges is not about denying or minimizing the difficulties we face. It is about acknowledging their existence while choosing to focus on the potential for growth and improvement. It is about recognizing that challenges are stepping stones to our ultimate success.

As entrepreneurs, we have the unique ability to transform problems into opportunities. By mastering the art of reframing, we unlock our full potential and pave the way for innovation and success. So, the next time you encounter a problem, take a deep breath, embrace the challenge, and embark on the journey of transforming it into an opportunity. Trust in your abilities, believe in your vision, and conquer the unknown with an unwavering spirit.

Now, as we reach the end of this chapter, we hope these insights have sparked a glimmer of hope and inspiration within you. But remember, this is only the beginning. In the second half of this chapter, we will delve deeper into practical strategies and case studies that exemplify the power of reframing. Get ready to uncover the secrets to turning your problems into opportunities, as we embark together on this transformative journey.

Remember, no matter how tough the road may seem, every problem is an opportunity in disguise – waiting for you to unravel its hidden treasures. So, until we meet again in the second half of this chapter, let the anticipation grow, and let the power of reframing guide you towards a future filled with limitless possibilities. Stay tuned for the next chapter, where we bring it all together and witness the magic of converting problems into opportunities. Now that we have explored the mindset and techniques of reframing problems as challenges, let us delve deeper into practical strategies and case studies that exemplify the power of this transformative approach. Prepare to be inspired as we uncover the secrets to turning your problems into opportunities.

One of the key strategies to reframe problems as challenges is to embrace the power of adaptability and flexibility. As entrepreneurs, we must understand that the business landscape is constantly evolving, and our ability to adapt to change is crucial for success. Instead of viewing unexpected circumstances as setbacks, see them as opportunities to pivot, innovate, and explore new directions.

Take, for example, the story of Sarah, a young entrepreneur who experienced a major setback when her manufacturing supplier could not deliver a crucial component on time for her product launch. Initially, Sarah was devastated and feared that this setback would tarnish her reputation and harm her business. However, instead of dwelling on the problem, she chose to reframe it as a challenge.

Sarah quickly reached out to her network and discovered a local supplier who could provide an alternative component. Although the new component was slightly different from her original design, Sarah embraced the opportunity to improve her product by incorporating this new feature. Not only did she meet the deadline, but her customers appreciated the upgraded version of her product, resulting in increased sales and positive word-of-mouth.

Another powerful strategy is that of collaboration and partnership. As entrepreneurs, it is easy to fall into a mindset of competition, viewing others in the industry as potential threats. However, by reframing this perspective, we can see our competitors as opportunities for collaboration and mutual growth.

Consider the example of Mark, a small business owner who ran a catering service. Instead of perceiving other caterers in his area as competitors, Mark saw them as potential partners. He reached out to them, offering his expertise in event planning and marketing, while seeking their assistance in expanding his reach. Through collaboration, Mark was able to tap into new markets, diversify his offerings, and build a strong network of supportive colleagues.

Additionally, the power of reframing can also be witnessed in the face of personal challenges. Entrepreneurs often face moments of self-doubt, discouragement, and burnout. Instead of succumbing to these negative emotions, we can reframe them as opportunities for personal growth and self-care.

Take the example of Lisa, a successful entrepreneur who experienced a period of burnout due to long hours and high stress. Instead of viewing burnout as a sign of weakness or failure, Lisa reframed it as an opportunity to prioritize her well-being and explore new ways of achieving work-life balance.

She implemented mindfulness and meditation practices into her daily routine, creating space for self-reflection and rejuvenation. Not only did she regain her energy and focus, but she also discovered new passions outside of work that brought her joy and fulfillment. This shift in mindset and self-care practices not only revitalized Lisa but also enhanced her creativity, productivity, and overall success.

As we conclude this chapter, remember that the power to reframe problems as challenges lies within you. By cultivating a positive mindset, analyzing problems from different perspectives, asking empowering questions, visualizing success, embracing experimentation, and surrounding yourself with a supportive network, you can transform any problem into an opportunity.

So, entrepreneurs, as you navigate the twists and turns of your entrepreneurial journey, remember that challenges are not roadblocks but stepping stones towards your ultimate success. Embrace the power of reframing, and let it guide you towards a future filled with limitless possibilities.

Thank you for joining us on this transformative journey. Stay tuned for the next chapters, where we will continue to explore the art of converting problems into opportunities. Until then, keep reframing and embracing the challenges that come your way, for within them lie the hidden treasures that will lead you to greatness.

Chapter 16: Leveraging Emotional Intelligence for Success

Emotional intelligence is a powerful tool that can provide entrepreneurs with a distinct advantage in navigating challenges, building strong relationships, and ultimately achieving sustainable success. In a world that often emphasizes technical skills and knowledge, the importance of emotional intelligence cannot be understated. It is a key component of effective leadership and can transform the way entrepreneurs approach their businesses and interact with others.

One of the fundamental aspects of emotional intelligence is self-awareness. Entrepreneurs who possess a high level of self-awareness have a deep understanding of their emotions, strengths, weaknesses, and values. They are able to recognize when they are experiencing stress or negative emotions, and they have the ability to manage these emotions effectively. Self-awareness enables entrepreneurs to make informed decisions, react to challenging situations with composure, and ultimately maintain resilience in the face of adversity.

Moreover, emotional intelligence allows entrepreneurs to develop empathy, which is another critical skill for success. Empathy is the ability to understand and share the feelings of others, enabling entrepreneurs to build strong and meaningful relationships with their employees, customers, and partners. By putting themselves in others' shoes, entrepreneurs can gain valuable insights, anticipate needs, and establish trust. This genuine connection with others not only fosters collaboration and teamwork, but it also enhances customer satisfaction and loyalty.

In addition to self-awareness and empathy, emotional intelligence equips entrepreneurs with the ability to manage their relationships effectively. As entrepreneurs, we often encounter challenges and conflicts that can strain our professional relationships. However, those with high emotional intelligence can navigate these situations with grace and diplomacy. They possess excellent interpersonal skills, which allow them to communicate clearly, listen actively, and resolve conflicts amicably. By maintaining open lines of communication and fostering a positive work environment, entrepreneurs can establish a culture of trust and cooperation within their organizations.

But emotional intelligence is not just about managing relationships with others; it also involves managing oneself. Entrepreneurs who possess emotional intelligence are adept at regulating their emotions and impulses, even when faced with immense pressure. They understand the importance of remaining composed and grounded, as it not only influences their decision-making but also sets an example for their teams. By maintaining emotional balance, entrepreneurs can make sound judgments, think critically, and adapt to changing circumstances effectively.

Moreover, emotional intelligence empowers entrepreneurs to convert setbacks into opportunities. Rather than viewing failures as insurmountable obstacles, emotionally intelligent entrepreneurs see them as valuable learning experiences. They embrace a growth mindset, understanding that challenges provide an opportunity for personal and professional development. This mindset allows entrepreneurs to bounce back from failures quickly, iterate their strategies, and ultimately come out stronger.

As entrepreneurs, we face countless challenges along our journey. The ability to leverage emotional intelligence is what sets the most successful ones apart. By developing self-awareness, empathy, and relationship management skills, entrepreneurs can build strong foundations for their businesses. They can foster a positive and inclusive work environment, establish meaningful connections with others, and navigate uncertainties with confidence. Emotional intelligence is not just a buzzword; it is a critical skill that can unlock endless opportunities for entrepreneurs.

NOTE: THIS CHAPTER will continue in the second half, exploring practical strategies for developing emotional intelligence and applying it in the entrepreneurial context. Stay tuned for the exciting conclusion in the next part! In the fast-paced and ever-changing world of entrepreneurship, emotional intelligence is a vital tool for achieving sustainable success. It empowers entrepreneurs to navigate challenges with grace, build strong relationships, and seize opportunities that others may overlook. In the first half of this chapter, we explored the fundamental aspects of emotional intelligence, including self-awareness, empathy, relationship management, and resilience. Now, let's delve deeper into practical strategies for developing and applying emotional intelligence in the entrepreneurial context.

To enhance self-awareness, entrepreneurs can engage in regular self-reflection and introspection. This could involve setting aside dedicated time each day to assess their emotions, thoughts, and reactions to various situations. By keeping a journal or practicing mindfulness techniques, entrepreneurs can deepen their understanding of their own strengths, weaknesses, triggers, and values. This self-awareness helps them make informed decisions, respond effectively to challenges, and maintain resilience in the face of adversity.

Empathy, the ability to understand and share the feelings of others, is a skill that can be cultivated through conscious effort. Entrepreneurs can actively work on developing empathy by actively listening to others, seeking to understand their perspectives, and practicing compassion.

Regularly engaging in activities that promote empathy, such as volunteering or participating in community service, can also strengthen this skill. As entrepreneurs, when we truly empathize with our employees, customers, and partners, we can build stronger relationships, foster collaboration, and enhance customer satisfaction.

Effective relationship management is not limited to external connections; it also involves managing oneself. Entrepreneurs with high emotional intelligence understand the importance of self-regulation, particularly in moments of intense pressure or conflict. By practicing techniques such as deep breathing, meditation, or taking short breaks to regain composure, entrepreneurs can manage their emotions and impulses effectively. This self-mastery sets an example for their teams and helps maintain a positive work environment.

Furthermore, emotionally intelligent entrepreneurs approach setbacks and failures with a growth mindset. Rather than dwelling on mistakes or viewing them as insurmountable obstacles, they see them as opportunities for growth. These resilient entrepreneurs cultivate a culture of continuous learning and improvement within their organizations. They encourage their teams to embrace failures as stepping stones to success, emphasizing that the most innovative ideas often emerge from the lessons learned through adversity.

Developing emotional intelligence requires practice and ongoing effort. Entrepreneurs can consider seeking feedback from trusted mentors, peers, or coaches to gain insights into their blind spots and areas for growth. Engaging in emotional intelligence training programs or workshops can also provide valuable tools and strategies for honing these skills.

Finally, remember that emotional intelligence is not a destination but an ongoing journey. It requires constant self-reflection, practice, and a willingness to adapt and learn from experiences. As entrepreneurs, we are constantly evolving, and so too should our emotional intelligence. By continually investing in developing emotional intelligence, we can create a solid foundation for our businesses and foster an environment that promotes sustainable success.

In conclusion, emotional intelligence is a powerful skill set that can empower entrepreneurs to overcome challenges, build strong relationships, and unlock endless opportunities. By developing self-awareness, empathy, and relationship management skills, entrepreneurs can navigate the entrepreneurial journey with confidence and resilience. Remember, success is not solely determined by technical skills and knowledge; emotional intelligence plays a vital role. As you embark on your entrepreneurial journey, embrace the power of emotional intelligence and discover the transformative impact it can have on your business and personal growth.

Congratulations on reaching the end of this chapter! Stay tuned for the next exciting installment, where we will explore another critical aspect of entrepreneurial success. Until then, keep cultivating emotional intelligence and harnessing its power to convert problems into opportunities.

Chapter 17: Fostering a Culture of Innovation

Innovation is the lifeblood of any entrepreneurial venture. It is the driving force that propels businesses forward, allows them to stay ahead of the competition, and paves the way for groundbreaking discoveries and advancements. As an entrepreneur, fostering a culture of innovation within your organization is not only imperative but also a strategic move that can lead to transformative growth and success.

Creating an environment that encourages and nurtures innovation begins with the mindset. It is crucial to establish a culture where failure is not feared but embraced as a valuable learning opportunity. Encouraging your team to take risks and explore new ideas without the fear of judgment or reprimand is instrumental in fostering an atmosphere of innovation.

One way to promote such a mindset is by highlighting and celebrating examples of successful innovations, both within your own venture and in the broader entrepreneurial landscape. Sharing stories of individuals who have overcome challenges and achieved remarkable breakthroughs can inspire and motivate your team to think creatively and push boundaries.

Another key aspect of fostering a culture of innovation is cultivating an open and collaborative work environment. Encourage your team members to freely exchange ideas, opinions, and perspectives. Embrace diversity within your organization, as it brings different experiences and backgrounds to the table, leading to a rich tapestry of innovative thinking.

Allowing for regular brainstorming sessions and collaborative problem-solving exercises can also be incredibly beneficial. Creating designated spaces or time slots for these activities can spark creativity and encourage the generation of fresh ideas. By involving employees from various departments and levels of expertise, you tap into a diverse pool of knowledge and unleash the full potential of your team.

To nurture innovation, it's essential to provide your team with the necessary resources and support. Allocate time and budget for research and development, allowing your employees to explore new concepts and experiment with different approaches. Provide access to training, workshops, and mentoring programs to enhance their skills and capabilities.

Empowering your team members to take ownership of their ideas fosters a sense of pride and ownership, ultimately driving their motivation to innovate. Encourage them to identify challenges and seek out opportunities for improvement or disruption. Create a framework where employees can pitch their ideas, and allocate resources to support the most promising ones.

Innovation thrives when there is a focus on continuous improvement. Encourage a mindset of constant learning and growth within your organization. Emphasize the importance of staying updated with industry trends, customer needs, and technological advancements. Foster a culture were staying ahead of the curve is not just an aspiration but a shared commitment.

By fostering a culture of innovation, you not only stimulate creativity and problem-solving within your organization but also attract and retain top talent. Entrepreneurs who prioritize innovation are seen as industry leaders and are more likely to attract like-minded individuals who thrive in a dynamic and forward-thinking environment.

Innovation is not a one-time endeavor, but a continuous journey. The first half of this chapter has explored various strategies to create an environment that fosters innovation within your entrepreneurial ventures. However, the journey does not end here. In the second half of this chapter, we will delve deeper into practical steps and case studies that exemplify how successful entrepreneurs have embraced innovation and overcome challenges.

Stay tuned for the second half of this chapter, where we will uncover the secrets to transforming obstacles into opportunities through innovative thinking and practices. Get ready to embrace a whole new perspective on turning challenges into triumphs. The power of innovation awaits you, entrepreneurs, and the best is yet to come.

In the second half of this chapter, we will dive deeper into practical steps and case studies that exemplify how successful entrepreneurs have embraced innovation and overcome challenges. These real-life examples will shed light on the power of innovative thinking and practices, inspiring you to unleash your own entrepreneurial potential.

One exceptional case study that demonstrates the transformative impact of fostering a culture of innovation is the story of Airbnb. Originally known as AirBed & Breakfast, the founders, Brian Chesky and Joe Gebbia, initially struggled to generate significant traction. However, fueled by their unwavering belief in the power of innovation, they persistently sought creative solutions to their challenges.

In 2008, faced with financial difficulties, the founders decided to rent out their own living space to travelers in need of accommodation. This simple act sparked an idea that would revolutionize the hospitality industry. They realized that people were willing to pay for a unique and authentic travel experience, and thus, Airbnb was born.

Through innovative thinking, Airbnb disrupted an established market, empowering individuals worldwide to monetize their spare rooms and providing travelers with a more intimate and cost-effective alternative to traditional hotels. This remarkable success story serves as a testament to the transformative power of embracing innovation and turning challenges into opportunities.

To emulate this kind of success, it is important to foster a mindset of continuous learning and improvement within your organization. Encourage your team members to explore emerging industry trends, embrace new technologies, and stay abreast of evolving customer needs. By continually adapting and evolving, you can ensure that your entrepreneurial ventures stay at the forefront of innovation.

Another vital aspect of cultivating a culture of innovation is to empower your team members to take ownership of their ideas and initiatives. One shining example of this can be seen in the rise of Elon Musk and his revolutionary electric vehicle company, Tesla. Musk not only created a groundbreaking product, but he also fostered a culture of innovation that empowered his employees to think creatively and challenge conventional wisdom.

At Tesla, individuals are encouraged to take risks and question the status quo. This approach has resulted in extraordinary feats of engineering and sparked innovations that have reshaped the entire automotive industry. By providing resources and support, Musk has created an environment that attracts top talent and allows them to bring their best ideas to fruition.

As an entrepreneur, it is equally important to recognize that innovation does not operate in a vacuum. Collaborative partnerships and industry alliances can play a pivotal role in fostering a culture of innovation. By forging connections with other entrepreneurs and like-minded individuals, you can tap into a network of diverse expertise and perspectives, leading to dynamic collaborations and breakthroughs.

One compelling example of this collaborative spirit can be seen in the world of technology, where industry giants like Google, Facebook, and Apple actively acquire smaller startups in order to integrate innovative technologies into their own offerings. This approach allows them to stay ahead of the curve and fuel continuous growth. By embracing collaboration, entrepreneurs can multiply their innovative potential and create a ripple effect throughout their ventures.

In conclusion, fostering a culture of innovation is not just a strategic move, but a fundamental aspect of entrepreneurial success. By embracing failure as a learning opportunity, cultivating a collaborative work environment, providing necessary resources and support, and continuously evolving and learning, you can create a powerful breeding ground for innovation within your organization.

The examples of Airbnb, Tesla, and other industry leaders demonstrate the extraordinary transformative power of innovative thinking and practices. By adopting an encouraging tone and inspiring fellow entrepreneurs to embrace a mindset of creativity, you have the ability to shape your own entrepreneurial journey and convert challenges into remarkable opportunities.

Remember, the power of innovation awaits you. Embrace a whole new perspective on turning challenges into triumphs, and let the entrepreneurial spirit guide you towards extraordinary achievements. Stay tuned for further chapters, where we'll delve deeper into other aspects of entrepreneurship, leaving no stone unturned in our quest for success. Keep pushing the boundaries and never stop innovating. You are on the path to greatness!

Chapter 18: Practicing Effective Problem-Solving Techniques

Problems. They can appear as obstacles blocking our path, as complications clouding our vision, or as challenges daring us to rise above them. For entrepreneurs, problems are an inevitable part of the journey towards success. However, it's not the problems themselves that define us; it's how we choose to tackle them head-on that sets us apart.

In this chapter, we will explore various problem-solving methodologies and techniques to effectively tackle challenges and create favorable outcomes. These powerful tools have been employed by successful entrepreneur's time and time again, enabling them to navigate the unpredictable landscape of business with confidence and resilience.

One such approach is the Five Whys technique, developed by Toyota's legendary Taiichi Ohno. It involves delving deep into the root causes of a problem by repeatedly asking "Why?" By peeling back the layers, we gain a holistic understanding of the issue at hand. This process not only addresses the immediate symptoms but also uncovers underlying factors that may have contributed to the problem's emergence. Embracing the Five Whys method allows entrepreneurs to address the core issues, leading to more sustainable and effective solutions.

Another valuable technique is brainstorming. By fostering an open and collaborative environment, entrepreneurs can harness the collective wisdom and creativity of their teams. Brainstorming sessions encourage individuals to voice their ideas, no matter how seemingly outrageous or unconventional they may be. Remember, innovation often springs from unexpected places. By embracing diverse perspectives and encouraging unrestricted thinking, entrepreneurs can uncover unique paths towards problem resolution.

Moreover, the Pareto principle, often dubbed the 80/20 rule, has proven to be a guiding light for entrepreneurs facing numerous challenges. This principle suggests that 80% of the effects stem from 20% of the causes. For instance, focusing on the vital few factors that yield the most significant impact can significantly streamline problem-solving efforts. By prioritizing key aspects, entrepreneurs can allocate their resources efficiently, driving tangible results and maximizing productivity.

An entrepreneurial mindset also involves thinking outside the box and turning traditional problem-solving approaches on their heads. Sometimes, the most effective solutions emerge from unexpected angles. Consider adopting the "reverse thinking" approach, in which you deliberately challenge the status quo and explore solutions contrary to conventional wisdom. Questioning assumptions and reframing problems may unveil innovative perspectives, ultimately leading to unconventional yet game-changing solutions.

In addition to these problem-solving methodologies, entrepreneurs must cultivate a mindset of opportunity amid adversity. Every setback presents an opportunity to learn, grow, and adapt. Rather than viewing problems as roadblocks, consider them as stepping stones towards success. Embrace the notion that failure can provide invaluable insights and course corrections, propelling you closer to your goals.

The entrepreneurial journey is fraught with uncertainties, but it is precisely these uncertainties that make it both exhilarating and rewarding. Challenges are not road signs telling you to turn back; they are invitations to push yourself further, to expand your horizons, and to transform problems into opportunities.

Now, as we conclude this chapter—just for now—remember that your entrepreneurial journey is an ongoing adventure. No problem is insurmountable if you approach it with the right mindset and employ effective problem-solving techniques. So, when faced with challenges, remember to dig deep with the Five Whys technique, leverage the power of collective brainstorming, apply the Pareto principle wisely, and dare to think differently.

Keep the flame of curiosity burning, and stay tuned for the second half of this chapter, where we will dive deeper into specific problem-solving strategies tailored to the needs of entrepreneurs. Remember, the path to success lies not in avoiding problems but in converting them into opportunities that propel you toward greatness. Embracing the strategies we have discussed thus far is only the beginning of your journey towards effective problem-solving as an entrepreneur. As you continue to navigate the ever-changing landscape of business, it is essential to delve deeper into specific problem-solving strategies tailor-made to address the unique needs and challenges you may encounter. In this second half of the chapter, we will explore additional techniques to further refine your problem-solving skills and empower you to create favorable outcomes.

One key strategy that successful entrepreneurs employ is known as the SWOT analysis. This acronym stands for Strengths, Weaknesses, Opportunities, and Threats. Conducting a comprehensive SWOT analysis enables you to gain a strategic understanding of your business or project by evaluating both internal and external factors. It helps identify areas where your strengths can be leveraged, weaknesses that need improvement, opportunities to be seized, and potential threats to be mitigated. By having a clear picture of your business's current state, you can better navigate challenges and make informed decisions that align with your goals.

Another valuable approach to problem-solving is known as the Six Thinking Hats technique, developed by Edward de Bono. This method encourages entrepreneurs to don different hats, metaphorically representing different perspectives or modes of thinking. Each hat represents a different approach, such as critical thinking, optimism, creativity, and risk assessment. By systematically wearing these different hats, you can explore a problem from various angles and foster well-rounded decision-making. This technique enhances collaboration and encourages individuals to challenge their own assumptions, leading to creative problem-solving and more comprehensive solutions.

Furthermore, the concept of failure should not be a deterrent but rather an opportunity for growth. Adopting a fail-forward mindset allows you to learn from past mistakes and course-correct effectively. Many successful entrepreneurs attribute their achievements to the lessons they learned from their failures. It is crucial to reframe setbacks as stepping stones rather than roadblocks on your path to success. Embrace the notion that challenges are not signs to turn away but invitations to push yourself further and unlock your full potential.

In addition to these techniques, fostering effective communication within your team is vital in problem-solving. As an entrepreneur, it is essential to create an environment where open dialogue thrives. Encourage your team members to voice their ideas and concerns, providing a platform for diverse perspectives to emerge. Effective communication ensures that everyone is aligned, and each team member feels valued and heard. Collaboration and innovation thrive in such an environment, leading to robust problem-solving and favorable outcomes.

Lastly, it is critical to cultivate resilience and adaptability as you face challenges along your entrepreneurial journey. Remember that setbacks are temporary, and success often lies just beyond them. Embrace a growth mindset, where challenges are viewed as opportunities for personal and professional development. Approach each obstacle with determination and a belief in your ability to find innovative solutions. Your resilience and adaptability will not only help you overcome current challenges but also equip you for future ones, allowing you to stay one step ahead in the dynamic world of business.

As we conclude this chapter, remember that effective problem-solving is an ongoing process. The techniques and strategies discussed here are meant to serve as your toolkit, enabling you to face challenges head-on and transform them into opportunities. Continuously seek knowledge, remain open to new ideas, and adapt your problem-solving approach as the business landscape evolves.

In the next chapter, we will dive deeper into the power of effective decision-making, exploring how to make informed and calculated choices that propel your entrepreneurial endeavors forward. Until then, embrace the spirit of perseverance, view challenges as opportunities, and remember that your journey towards greatness is built on your ability to convert problems into stepping stones towards success.

Chapter 19: Aligning Purpose and Passion with Challenges

In the journey of entrepreneurship, challenges are inevitable. They present themselves in various forms, testing our determination and resilience. Yet, hidden within these trials lies the potential for growth and transformation. By aligning our purpose and passion with the challenges we face, we unlock a powerful force that propels us towards greater fulfillment and success.

Understanding the importance of aligning purpose and passion with challenges is a gateway to unlocking our true potential. When our endeavors are driven by a deep-rooted purpose, fueled by a burning passion, we are more likely to navigate turbulent waters with tenacity and grace. Purpose ignites our inner fire, inspiring us to persevere even when the path ahead seems daunting.

Discovering our purpose goes beyond simply identifying our goals or ambitions. It is a profound process of introspection and self-discovery that requires delving into the depths of our true selves. As entrepreneurs, it is crucial to ask ourselves the meaningful questions that illuminate our purpose. What impact do we wish to make? Whose lives do we aim to touch? Understanding the why behind our entrepreneurial pursuits infuses our actions with purpose and ensures our efforts are aligned with our authentic selves.

Passion, on the other hand, is the fuel that drives us forward. It is the fervent energy that ignites our hearts and souls. Passion fuels our determination, bringing color to our lives and infusing our work with enthusiasm. When we pursue our passions, we find ourselves immersed in a world where our work doesn't feel like a burden; instead, it becomes a source of joy and inspiration.

The magic truly happens when we align our purpose and passion with the challenges that arise on our entrepreneurial journey. Challenges can often seem insurmountable, leaving us feeling overwhelmed and discouraged. However, when we view these obstacles through the lens of purpose and passion, they become lessons in disguise. We become aware that behind every challenge lies an opportunity for growth, innovation, and self-discovery.

Aligning purpose and passion with challenges brings about a shift in our perspective. Rather than viewing difficulties as roadblocks, we see them as stepping stones towards our ultimate vision. Each roadblock presents an opportunity to refine our purpose, reignite our passion, and realign our actions to propel us closer to our goals. Challenges unveil our true character, forcing us to dig deep within ourselves to find the strength and resilience needed to overcome them.

Furthermore, aligning purpose and passion with our challenges does not only benefit us individually; it also has a ripple effect on those around us. As entrepreneurs, we have the power to inspire, motivate, and empower others. When we face challenges with unwavering purpose and passion, we become beacons of hope for those who may be struggling. Our journey becomes a testament to the possibilities that await when we align our inner desires with our external circumstances.

In the midst of our entrepreneurial endeavors, we must remember that challenges are not setbacks; they are stepping stones to growth and personal evolution. With purpose and passion as our driving forces, we can navigate through the ever-changing landscape of entrepreneurship with unwavering determination. Our challenges become catalysts for transformation, propelling us towards a future where success and fulfillment go hand in hand.

As you continue to read this chapter, you will find valuable insights and practical strategies to help you align your purpose and passion with the challenges you face. By embracing the power of intention and igniting the flame of passion within you, you will be better equipped to navigate through the twists and turns of the entrepreneurial journey. Get ready to embark on a transformative adventure, where challenges become opportunities, and success becomes an inevitable outcome. With purpose and passion as our guiding forces, we can now delve deeper into practical strategies that will help us align our purpose and passion with the challenges we face as entrepreneurs.

One important strategy is to approach challenges as opportunities for growth and learning. Instead of being intimidated or discouraged by obstacles, view them as stepping stones that will shape you into a stronger and more resilient entrepreneur. Embrace the mindset that every challenge is an invitation to expand your skills, knowledge, and capabilities. Embracing a growth mindset allows you to see challenges as opportunities to improve and evolve, rather than as roadblocks that hinder progress.

Next, take the time to reflect on your purpose and passion and how they align with the specific challenges you encounter. Ask yourself how your purpose aligns with the challenge at hand and how your passion fuels your determination to overcome it. When you are clear about the why behind your entrepreneurial pursuits and deeply connected to your passions, it becomes easier to stay focused and motivated in the face of adversity.

In addition, seek support and guidance from mentors, coaches, or like-minded individuals who can provide valuable insights and perspectives. Surround yourself with individuals who share your values and can offer guidance based on their experiences. Learning from others who have faced similar challenges can provide invaluable advice and support that will help you navigate the entrepreneurial journey with confidence and resilience.

Furthermore, adopt a problem-solving mindset that allows you to see challenges as opportunities to innovate and create. Instead of getting overwhelmed by the difficulties, approach them as chances to find creative solutions and think outside the box. Embrace the belief that every problem has a solution waiting to be discovered and that you have the capability to find it. By approaching challenges with a positive and solution-oriented mindset, you empower yourself to overcome them and thrive.

It is also important to maintain self-care practices during challenging times. Taking care of your physical, mental, and emotional well-being is crucial for maintaining the resilience and energy needed to overcome obstacles. Engage in activities that bring you joy and relaxation, such as exercise, meditation, hobbies, or spending time with loved ones. By taking care of yourself, you replenish your inner resources and strengthen your ability to face challenges head-on.

Lastly, remember that setbacks are a natural part of the entrepreneurial journey. Embrace failures and mistakes as valuable learning opportunities. Celebrate the lessons learned and use them to refine your purpose, reignite your passion, and realign your actions. Remember that every successful entrepreneur has faced their fair share of challenges and setbacks along the way. It is through these experiences that they have grown, developed resilience, and achieved success.

As you move forward on your entrepreneurial journey, keep in mind that challenges are not setbacks but opportunities for growth and personal evolution. By aligning your purpose and passion with the challenges you face, you embody the true spirit of entrepreneurship. With unwavering determination, resilience, and optimism, you will overcome obstacles and achieve remarkable success.

In conclusion, aligning purpose and passion with challenges is the ultimate recipe for entrepreneurial fulfillment and success. By embracing the power of intention and fueling your actions with the flame of passion, you will navigate through the twists and turns of entrepreneurship with grace and tenacity. Challenges will no longer be roadblocks but stepping stones on your path to growth and personal evolution. So, take a deep breath, trust in your purpose, ignite your passion, and let the transformation begin. Embrace the opportunities that lie within your challenges and unleash your full potential as an entrepreneur. The world is waiting for you to shine.

Chapter 20: Celebrating Success and Appreciating the Journey

As an entrepreneur, the journey towards success can often feel like a rollercoaster ride. It is filled with ups and downs, challenges, and obstacles that test your resilience and determination. However, it is important to recognize and appreciate the milestones achieved along the way. In this chapter, we reflect on the significance of celebrating success and acknowledging the importance of the journey itself.

Every entrepreneur starts with a vision, a dream to create something meaningful and impactful. However, the path to turning that vision into reality is not always smooth. It is easy to get caught up in the daily struggles of running a business, constantly chasing after new goals, and forgetting to take a step back to appreciate how far you have come.

Celebrating success is not just about throwing a lavish party or boasting about your achievements. It is about acknowledging the efforts, perseverance, and dedication that you have invested in your entrepreneurial journey. Whether it is reaching a certain revenue milestone, launching a new product, or receiving recognition from your peers, taking the time to celebrate creates a positive and uplifting atmosphere within your organization.

Recognizing achievements not only boosts morale but also fosters a sense of accomplishment and purpose among your team members. When employees feel valued and appreciated, they become motivated to work harder, contribute their best efforts, and go above and beyond to achieve even greater milestones. Celebrating success together creates a culture of positivity and unity, strengthening the bond within the entrepreneurial community.

Moreover, celebrations act as reminders of how overcoming challenges and embracing the journey have shaped you as an entrepreneur. The obstacles you have faced and the failures you have experienced are stepping stones towards growth and resilience. Each setback and lesson learned is a valuable part of the journey, contributing to your personal and professional development.

Appreciating the journey is not just about the destination, but the experiences, lessons, and personal growth that come along with it. Reflecting on the challenges faced and the lessons learned along the way can inspire and motivate you to keep pushing forward, even during the toughest times. Embrace the hurdles as opportunities for growth and transformation, gradually transforming challenges into opportunities.

The entrepreneurial journey is a constant learning process. It is crucial to embrace the learning moments and appreciate the progress made, regardless of the outcome. Cultivate a mindset that perceives setbacks and failures as valuable lessons rather than insurmountable obstacles. By doing so, you can approach challenges with a fresh perspective, finding innovative solutions and pushing the boundaries of your entrepreneurial endeavors.

As an entrepreneur, celebrating success and appreciating the journey is not only beneficial for you but also essential for your team and overall business growth. Take the time to reflect on your achievements, no matter how big or small, and express gratitude for every step of the journey. This positivity will radiate within your organization, attracting like-minded individuals who are passionate about the same goals and aspirations.

Remember, success is not strictly measured by monetary gains or external recognition but by the knowledge gained, the improvements made, and the impact created. Celebrate the milestones, acknowledge your achievements, and appreciate the journey as an entrepreneur. By doing so, you will create an environment that thrives on positivity, continuous growth, and the relentless pursuit of excellence.

As we wrap up this first half of the chapter, let us take a moment to reflect on the successes we have achieved thus far. The journey has been challenging, yet we have overcome numerous obstacles, pushed our limits, and reach milestones we once deemed impossible. But, dear entrepreneurs, this is just the beginning. In the second half of this chapter, we will delve deeper into the practices and strategies that can help us cultivate a culture of celebration and appreciation within our entrepreneurial endeavors. Stay tuned for the exciting insights that lie ahead! In the second half of this chapter, we will dive deeper into the practical strategies and practices that can cultivate a culture of celebration and appreciation within our entrepreneurial endeavors. These insights will help us not only recognize and acknowledge our achievements but also inspire us to further embrace the journey towards success.

One of the key practices to celebrate success is to create a supportive and uplifting environment within your organization. As entrepreneurs, it is crucial to lead by example and foster a culture where accomplishments are celebrated and efforts are appreciated. Encourage your team members to share their successes and milestones, whether big or small. By creating a space for open dialogue, you not only celebrate individual achievements but also inspire others to strive for greatness.

Another powerful strategy is to establish a regular system for recognizing and rewarding accomplishments. This can be done through employee appreciation programs, where individuals are publicly recognized and rewarded for their contributions. Celebrate milestones such as hitting revenue targets, launching successful campaigns, or achieving significant growth. By acknowledging these achievements, you not only boost morale but also create a sense of pride and motivation among your team members.

In addition to recognizing external accomplishments, it is equally important to celebrate personal growth and development. Encourage your team members to set personal goals and milestones within their professional journey. This can be completing a certification, mastering a new skill, or overcoming a personal challenge. By celebrating personal growth, you create a culture that values continuous learning and empowers individuals to constantly improve themselves.

Furthermore, do not underestimate the power of regular team-building activities and bonding experiences. These activities not only provide an opportunity to celebrate success but also strengthen the relationships within your team. Organize team outings, workshops, or even virtual events where members can come together, connect, and celebrate the journey as a collective. These moments of celebration and appreciation build a sense of camaraderie, teamwork, and unity, creating an environment that thrives on collaboration and mutual support.

It is also essential to remember the importance of gratitude during the entrepreneurial journey. Take the time to express gratitude towards your team members, partners, clients, and supporters who have been instrumental in your successes. A simple thank you or a handwritten note can go a long way in showing appreciation and fostering meaningful connections. Gratitude not only strengthens relationships but also attracts positive energy and opportunities into your entrepreneurial journey.

Finally, as entrepreneurs, it is crucial to celebrate your own achievements and appreciate the personal growth you have experienced. Take a moment to reflect on how far you have come and the challenges you have overcome. Acknowledge the lessons learned from failures and setbacks, as they have contributed to your growth and resilience. By celebrating your own journey, you inspire others to embrace their own challenges and transform them into opportunities.

Dear entrepreneurs, as we conclude this chapter, let us remember that celebrating success and appreciating the journey is not just a one-time event but an ongoing mindset. By continuously recognizing achievements, fostering a supportive environment, and expressing gratitude, we create a culture that encourages resilience, innovation, and growth.

May this chapter serve as a reminder to celebrate every milestone, big or small, and appreciate the journey as entrepreneurs. The road to success may be filled with twists and turns, but it is within these moments of celebration and reflection that we find the fuel to keep pushing forward.

Now go forth, dear entrepreneurs, and continue to convert your problems into opportunities. Embrace the challenges, appreciate the journey, and celebrate your successes. The world is waiting for the impact you are destined to create.

Disclaimer

The information provided in this book is for general informational and educational purposes only and is not intended as a substitute for professional advice, diagnosis, or treatment. The author and publisher have made every effort to ensure the accuracy and reliability of the information provided within these pages, but they make no guarantees, either express or implied, regarding the content's completeness, accuracy, or applicability.

Neither the author nor the publisher shall be held liable or responsible for any misunderstanding or misuse of the information contained in this book or for any loss, damage, or injury caused, or alleged to be caused, directly or indirectly by any treatment, action, or application of any advice discussed in this publication. The statements made within this book are not intended to diagnose, treat, cure, or prevent any disease. Readers should consult with a qualified healthcare provider for medical advice tailored to their personal circumstances.

The views and opinions expressed herein are those of the author alone and do not necessarily reflect the official policy or position of any agency or company. All content provided in this book is on an "as-is" basis and the author and publisher disclaim all responsibility for any errors or omissions.

Don't miss out!

Visit the website below and you can sign up to receive emails whenever Gonzalo Estrada publishes a new book. There's no charge and no obligation.

https://books2read.com/r/B-A-OZBBB-BRJZC

BOOKS2READ

Connecting independent readers to independent writers.

Did you love *Transform Your Problems into Opportunities*? Then you should read *The Art of Cosmic Connection*[1] by Gonzalo Estrada!

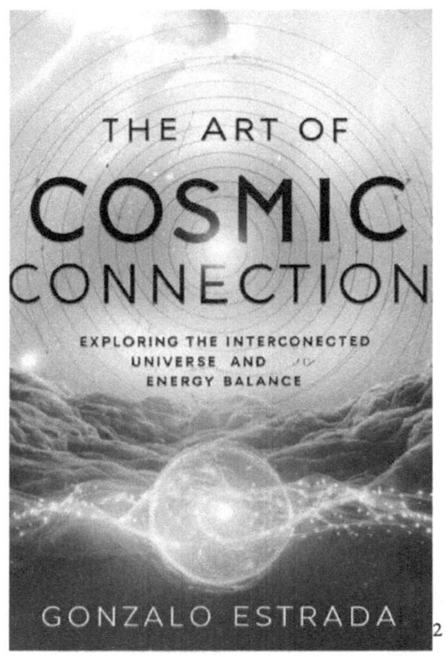

Embark on a transformative journey with "The Art of Cosmic Connection: Exploring the Interconnected Universe and Energy Balance." This enlightening book by Gonzalo Estrada guides you through the profound realization that we are all part of a grand, interconnected cosmos. Each chapter delves into different facets of our universal bond, from the awakening of cosmic consciousness to the intricate dance of energy cycles influenced by celestial bodies.

Discover the power of intuition and how it can open doors to healing and understanding. Learn to harness the energy of relationships to maintain balance in your life. Explore the wisdom of ancient traditions and how they can inform our modern existence.

---

1. https://books2read.com/u/47vn77

2. https://books2read.com/u/47vn77

Through meditation, introspection, and creative visualization, you'll find ways to align with the universe's energy for a more harmonious life.

"The Art of Cosmic Connection" is more than a book; it's a guide to living authentically, embracing the present, and understanding the purpose of life through the lens of cosmic connectivity. Whether you're drawn to the arts, the power of speech, or the resonance of music and sound, this book offers insights into how these elements can enhance your spiritual and energetic alignment.

Join Gonzalo Estrada in uncovering the secrets of the universe and learn how to live in harmony with its infinite energy. This book is an essential read for anyone seeking to deepen their understanding of the cosmos and their place within it.

Also by Gonzalo Estrada

Self Healing
Visualiza tu Éxito
Cultivando Líderes
Afirmaciones y Empoderamiento
Semillas de Cambio
Cómo convertir TikTok en una máquina de hacer dinero
Cómo hacer dinero con Pinterest
Cómo hacer un ensayo
Cómo Pedir un Aumento de Sueldo
Currículo Poderoso
Entrenamiento sin Violencia
Entrevista Laboral
Gana Dinero con X (Twitter)
Ganar Masa Muscular
Volver a Empezar; el arte de reinventarse
Analiza Resuelve Ejecuta
Aromatherapy, The natural path to your pet´s well being
Holistic Feeding
The ABC of Educating Your Pet
The Art of Cosmic Connection
The Art of Feng Shui applied to your Pets
From Scarcity to Abundance
The English Bulldog in The Family
The French Bulldog
Therapeutic Massages for Pets

Pets and Crystal Therapy
The Maltese Bichon
Transform Your Problems into Opportunities

About the Author

Gonzalo Estrada is a prolific and renowned author, whose books cover topics that resonate with humanity. With a prominent presence in both physical and online media, Estrada has made a significant mark in contemporary literature. His works, of great significance on platforms such as Amazon, Barnes & Noble, and many others, reflect his deep knowledge and passion for the subjects he tackles. From the transformative power of gratitude to the unique personality of the French Bulldog, Estrada has proven to be a versatile and captivating writer who has connected with readers from all over the world.